# Discernment in Christian Initiation

Donna Steffen, SC

LTP
LITURGY
TRAINING
PUBLICATIONS

*Nihil Obstat*
Reverend Mr. Daniel G. Welter, JD
Chancellor
Archdiocese of Chicago
May 30, 2018

*Imprimatur*
Very Reverend Ronald A. Hicks
Vicar General
Archdiocese of Chicago
May 30, 2018

The *Nihil Obstat* and Imprimatur are declarations that the material is free from doctrinal or moral error, and thus is granted permission to publish in accordance with c. 827. No legal responsibility is assumed by the grant of this permission. No implication is contained herein that those who have granted the *Nihil Obstat* and Imprimatur agree with the content, opinions, or statements expressed.

DISCERNMENT IN CHRISTIAN INITIATION © 2018 Archdiocese of Chicago: Liturgy Training Publications, 3949 South Racine Avenue, Chicago, IL 60609; 800-933-1800; fax 800-933-7094; email: orders@ltp.org; website: www.LTP.org. All rights reserved.

The two previous editions of this book were titled *Discerning Disciples: Listening for God's Voice in Christian Initiation*.

This book was edited by Mary Fox. Víctor R. Pérez was the production editor, Juan Alberto Castillo was the designer, and Luis Leal was the production artist.

Cover art from Shutterstock.

22  21  20  19  18      1  2  3  4  5

Printed in the United States of America.

Library of Congress Control Number: 2018949297

ISBN 978-1-61671-433-8

DCI

# Contents

*Foreword*     *iv*
*Introduction*      *vi*

Chapter 1: Disciples Discern       1
Chapter 2: The Discernment Process        6
Chapter 3: The Way of Discerning Listening        20
Chapter 4: Discernment in the Precatechumenate        35
Chapter 5: Discernment in the Catechumenate Period        47
Chapter 6: Discernment during Purification and Enlightenment        59
Chapter 7: Mystagogia and Beyond        68
Chapter 8: The Baptized Candidate        73
Chapter 9: Discernment with Children        84
Chapter 10: Initiation Ministers        95

*Appendix 1: The Initial Interview        105*
*Appendix 2: The Interview during the Precatechumenate        107*
*Appendix 3: The First Interview during the Catechumenate        110*
*Appendix 4: The Interview before the Rite of Election        112*
*Appendix 5: The Discernment Day before the Rite of Election        115*
*Appendix 6: The Training of Team Members and
             Sponsors in the Way of Discerning Listening        119*

*Notes        125*
*Bibliography        127*

# Foreword

Christians who walk the path of discipleship are on a spiritual journey immersed in reflecting on the Paschal Mystery, which leads them to faithful living and service. Integral to faithful discipleship is discernment. Though discernment may often seem too time consuming in a fast-paced world, God's desire for our lives is discovered by quietly listening to his voice as we prayerfully approach decisions, opportunities, and challenges. Discernment enables us to center our lives in Christ as it calls us to a deeper awareness of the inner voices that shape who we are and how we choose to live.

*Discernment in Christian Initiation*, titled *Discerning Disciples* in its two previous editions, has become a classic for Christian initiation ministers. Its author, Sr. Donna Steffen, SC, provides a spiritual compass for Christian initiation ministers with adults and children of catechetical age. Sr. Donna, a specialist in Christian initiation, a spiritual director, and a woman of prayer, inspires initiation ministers, godparents, and sponsors to become discerning disciples themselves as they accompany others on their journey to Christ and his Church.

Through her understanding and experience, Sr. Donna explores discernment and provides a theological basis for the essential role it plays in the life of all disciples. In addition, she outlines the skills necessary for initiation ministers to assist catechumens and candidates as they discern their path of discipleship. Perhaps most notable of these skills are her suggestions for "discerning listening," the ability to listen to another's story while avoiding typical pitfalls and challenges. The Christian initiation minister will find that these discernment skills will not only strengthen their work in pastoral care but will be valuable in all of their relationships.

In addition, this book provides a clear and comprehensive examination of discernment throughout the Christian initiation process. Sr. Donna focuses on the key moments of discernment as envisioned by the rite and highlights the specific signs of conversion that help the Church and the discerning disciple to recognize the movement of the Holy Spirit as they prepare to take the next step on their journey. The last chapters address particular circumstances such as discernment with children and with the already baptized. Finally, and not to be missed, the appendices include extremely practical interview tools that are helpful to initiation ministers throughout the discernment process.

In my more than twenty years of diocesan initiation experience in the Archdiocese of Cincinnati, I have found this book to be one of the most practical initiation resources available. Equally important, Sr. Donna has captured in her writing how to walk the path of faith with others, leading them into an ever deeper relationship with Christ and his Church. This book is a must for all initiation ministers.

Karen Kane

Director of the Office of Divine Worship

and Sacraments for the Archdiocese of Cincinnati

# Introduction

Since the beginning of my involvement in parish Christian initiation ministry, I have grown in appreciation of discernment in the initiation process. When I first attended a workshop on discernment as part of the *Rite of Christian Initiation of Adults*, I was horrified at the thought. As we looked at case studies and ways of determining who was ready to be initiated and who should wait, I could not imagine asking someone to delay initiation. I thought, "Who are we on parish staffs to play God and decide what is in another's heart and what God wants for that person?"

After twenty-three years of parish experience with initiation, and twenty-nine years of doing spiritual direction since my internship in this ministry, I have been converted to the notion of discernment in the process of initiation. Both the experience of initiation with real people with very real lives, and my awareness of how God speaks through the truth as it is manifest in a person's life, have been significant teachers for me. As I write, I think of the people who have given meaning to the question of discernment in initiation. I think of Kathy, age thirty-three, who wanted to be baptized but said she could not come to the Vigil because she had to stay home and cook dinner for her husband. What is the truth and what are all the underlying situations implied in such a statement? We made a pastoral decision to baptize her at Mass on Pentecost. She seemed filled with much anger, and we did not want to turn her away. At her funeral less than two years later, we learned from her parents how she, with seemingly little support from her husband, was intent on Baptism as she dealt with her breast cancer somewhat alone. I think of Jeremy, who did all the right things, had a Catholic wife and children, was initiated, and who subsequently attended Mass only on Christmas and Easter. I think of Carol who, after her initiation became involved in children's religious formation, later became coordinator of initiation ministry in the parish, and eventually took my place as pastoral associate. I think of Jackie, who after her Baptism, said to her husband, "This is even deeper than my marriage vows." I think of John, a friend and carpenter, who attended Mass with his wife for twenty-five years, and whose life was forever changed through what he experienced in this process. I think of Mary, a practicing Lutheran, who went to two parishes to see about "becoming Catholic" during her time of marriage preparation, and was told in one place to "come back in September" and in another, "you don't need anything," while having her own sense of what she needed. I think of eight-year-old Frank, who would not take a bath for a week after the Easter Vigil. He was so proud of the smell of Chrism in his hair, that he wanted his classmates to "smell him" upon their return to school after spring break. I think of many others as well.

How does discernment fit in with these stories and the stories of the people you know? I have come to understand that whether it is named or unnamed, there is a truth of how God is acting in the lives of these individuals. Discernment has to do with acknowledging and talking about this truth in a person's heart and life, in this case with respect to the initiation process. At times, we are more or less successful in naming the truth and talking about it with the inquirer, catechumen, candidate, adult, or child. But the truth is there within the person. Often, there is a hesitancy on the part of initiation ministers to talk with the person about deeper and real issues. As I do initiation workshops locally, in various dioceses, and in the past with the North American Forum on the Catechumenate, I often have heard the question, "What do we do when . . . ?" My first response is, "Talk to him or her. The sooner, the better." We sense when something is going on with the person but somehow hold back from talking about it.

Pastoral practice has shown me that inner truth often manifests itself outwardly and is better talked about than not. This is different from a distant judgment of who fits the bill and who does not. It is, instead, a closer looking at what is there. My experience is that when we sit and talk and listen with someone, that person will usually reveal a deeper level of what is occurring inside. We talk and relate in truth. The initiation process invites all of us who are involved with it to this level of true relationship.

Discernment is a frequently used word. At times, it is used by many in much the same way as I first understood it: as a decision-making process. People frequently say, "We have to discern that." What many really mean is that they want to make a good decision. Decision-making is different from discernment. The two are not in opposition, but they arise out of a different place within the person. Discernment is not so much a rational process, but a listening to what God is doing, to where God is leading. Discernment involves holding the truth of what is within the person open-heartedly before God. Then the way forward and its timing will be given.

Truly doing discernment presupposes that initiation in the local parish occur in a year-round process—the precatechumenate takes as long as needed, with movement to the catechumenate when the person is ready. The catechumenate also takes as long as necessary. Of course, the Rite of Election and the sacraments of initiation generally are celebrated at fixed times.

This book discusses the meaning of discernment in real life. In the second edition, the description of discerning listening was embellished from the earlier edition. Discernment in the various stages of ministry with the unbaptized person is described. Then, this book explores discernment as it relates to the situations of the baptized catechized and baptized uncatechized candidates. Dimensions of catechesis are described. Discernment is necessary to determine how catechized a person is, whether conversion has occurred, and if it has, what more is needed for the person to live as a full member of the Catholic community.[1] Each person who comes our way, no matter what category he or she fits into, is unique. Discernment is needed to determine the appropriate formation.

Discernment in the initiation of children is addressed. Some specific areas for consideration and dimensions of conversion as it is evidenced in children are highlighted. Coordinators and catechists working with children will benefit from further resources in gleaning ways of doing initiation ministry with children.

Areas of discernment for initiation ministers are presented. Initiation ministry belongs to the whole parish. However, in each local situation some specific people hold a large part of the responsibility for initiation ministry. This book explores various dimensions of discernment in the parish, in personal life, and in the lives of the initiation ministers. God acts in the lives of the ministers, as well as in the lives of catechumens and candidates. Discernment is often needed in taking a next step toward moving out of stuck places in initiation ministers, in more fully developing their faith life, and in fostering an initiation process according to the rite's vision.

The following chapters will explore more fully what discernment is and what it might look like in real lives. I will offer specific skills for discernment with others. The necessity of discernment in the lives of all true disciples is the foundation for discernment with those being initiated. The role of discernment in the *Rite of Christian Initiation of Adults* is the basis for understanding discernment in adult initiation ministry.

To help make the transition from words about discernment to how it looks in human experience, I use specific examples of people I know. However, the names have been changed.

Reflection questions at the end of each chapter are to assist readers in becoming aware of various aspects of discernment within themselves and in the parish where they are ministering. The appendices provide specific outlines for various interviews, offer a discernment process for use before the Rite of Election, and suggest a possible way of training team members and sponsors in the way of discerning listening. These offerings may be used as written, or adapted in a way fitting the local parish situation. It is hoped that these tools will be a springboard for more processes of discernment to develop.

All believers in Christ are invited to live as discerning disciples, which does not mean that all disciples are gifted with the art of spiritual direction. Spiritual directors are trained in an understanding of the spiritual life and in the art of discernment, which has different characteristics in various movements of the spiritual life. This book presents a basic understanding of discernment. I consistently name those doing discernment with others in this initiation process as *discerning listeners* rather than using the title of spiritual director. As one who is trained and is involved in the training of others in the ministry of spiritual direction, I know it to be a profession that includes skill as well as a gift. An understanding of the movements of the spiritual life and specific concerns of discernment within these movements is necessary and beyond what this book offers. Usually, the learning needed to engage in the ministry of spiritual direction involves reflection on material in relationship to one's life experience and life of relationship with God. The ministry of spiritual direction is also grounded in one's learning as a recipient of spiritual direction. Training in this ministry includes feedback given while being observed in performing spiritual direction, and paying attention in supervision to one's areas of strength and ways of lacking freedom in this in this ministry. I believe the title of spiritual director ought not to be used or given without specific professional training. But there is still a level of discernment available to and needed by those of us who are disciples and who work in initiation ministry. This discernment is the focus of the following pages.

I invite you to come along on this journey. Bring your life experience, your personality and heart, as well as the stories of those whom you have been privileged to accompany through their initiation process. For, as any of you who work with initiation know, when we accompany others on their journey we are also converted, over and over, and more and more deeply. Our beliefs and understandings shift as our lives become God's playground. I invite you to read this book with your mind and your heart and your whole being.

We believe in an incarnational God. God truly is alive and acts in our real life experience. Discernment in our lives and in initiation ministry can be just an ideal. It is you, the initiation minister, who puts flesh on discernment and makes it real in your parish. You, and others with you, are entrusted with this sacred ministry.

Donna Steffen, sc
October 23, 2017

# Chapter 1

# Disciples Discern

## We Follow One Who Discerns

Why is discernment essential in initiation processes? There are several layers of response to this question.

We begin with the level of identity: who we are and what we are about. We the Church, the community of believers, are disciples of Jesus the Christ. Discipleship involves living with and in the being of Christ. We believe in Jesus Christ. More than knowing about Christ, we know the person. Our heart knows the heart of Christ. We know Christ in the many aspects of his life: one who walked and talked with others; who invited, called, and sent out; who healed and liberated and ate meals; who at times challenged religious authorities and who also spoke with authority. We know the heart of this person who believed until death and beyond in the Holy One, the God who is faithful and full of limitless love. We know this Jesus who was so deeply connected with God, even in his human nature, that he always lived out of this relationship. Jesus opted to live as "the chosen one, the beloved." Jesus always based his life on love, goodness, truth, on the Holy One, rather than pride, power over, or sin. We clearly see Jesus listening to the Spirit, discerning God's way, in the scene of the temptations in the desert (Matthew 4:1–11). Jesus discerns. When God's way becomes clear, Jesus chooses it. Until his death, Jesus continues choosing God's way rather than hatred and evil. It is this Jesus of whom we, the baptized, are disciples. So we too must choose the ways of our loving, faithful God, even in the face of hatred, pain, and death.

## Good and Evil Choices

Before we can choose God's way, we must first know which way, direction, or choice is of God. God's way is often clearer when the choice is between good and evil. When discerning choices, people usually do not speak of them as being between good and evil. If we listen carefully, it is the reality of what they are saying. The evil or sin spoken of, as well as the good they moved toward, has to do with broader understandings or patterns that involve a way of life or a world view. In general, people name this movement from evil to good as some change, or change in direction in their life. They may make statements such as

- "I was not a nice person. I just lived for myself. But I felt empty. Now I have another way of looking at life."

- "My husband works for the justice system. All kinds of people come through there, and he seems to understand more about them and their lives than I do. I used to just look down at them and think, 'Why can't they just do the right thing like they're supposed to?' I'm now able to stop judging so much and see others as people. I have more understanding that the home they were raised in is different from what I had growing up. I realize how I was always very hard on myself, too."

- "I used to just mind my own business. I took care of myself and let others take care of themselves. I have my own responsibilities. Let them take care of theirs. Now, we've just taken in a cousin's young pregnant daughter. If you told me three years ago I would have done this, I would have told you you were crazy."

## The Illusion of Good

Evil also can be masked as an "angel of light," as Ignatius would say.[1] What is perceived as a good is not really good. The illusory good does not really bring about true life. For example: "I used to be very work-oriented so that I could make more money to buy my son all of the right kinds of toys and clothes. Now I'm spending more time with him. I know he needs me more than things."

## Two Good Choices

But often the discernment is between two good choices. Then the question becomes "Where is God's invitation to me?" For example, is God inviting me to spend more time with my family or to work with initiation ministry? Is it better to bring up a problem with my neighbor and talk about it or let it go? How do I know, or *discern*? Am I to speak out about an injustice at work and risk losing my job when my family depends on my income? What is God's invitation? How am I to deal with an in-law problem, alcoholism, or an illness? What is God's call? Where is the call of God as I come to claim my sexual orientation as homosexual for the first time or when I realize I can no longer be part of an abusive marriage? The underlying assumption is that God is active in all parts of real-life experience. God has a will, or dream, or call for each of us in our real experiences that will bring about a deeper wholeness and a closer relationship with God.

## Disciples Discern

Discernment is an integral part in the life of all disciples. In order to be discipled, formed into Christians, those bearing the name of Christ, we must live the way of discernment. The beginning place for discernment for those working with the initiation process is within our own lives. We are called to be disciples who are continually discerning God's call and invitation to us in the concrete aspects of our lives.

## Disciples Hand on the Way of Discernment

As disciples, we are also about the ministry of discerning with others whether they, too, at this time of their lives, are called into discipleship within this particular faith community. In the initiation process we are not about discerning for others whether they belong or whether the timing is right for them. Rather, we discern *with* them.

Part of our ministry as discerning disciples ourselves is the formation of other discerning disciples. The way of discernment is passed on to those being initiated by discerning with them and by the examples of our own lives. By living the way of discernment we teach them to be discerning. Discernment is an essential part of the way of discipleship we want others to take on as they become disciples or deepen their discipleship.

As we look at discernment in the various stages or movements of the initiation process, it is important to keep in our vision this larger picture of discernment. Its whole context involves living our lives as disciples who discern, and forming other disciples who discern. Discernment is essential to who we are and how we live as Church, as well as to initiating other disciples.

## Discernment Is Necessary in Initiation

Discernment is also made necessary by the theology and celebration of the Rite of Christian Initiation of Adults. Each of the stages tells us what the marks of spiritual development are of that particular period. The sections on the rites describe what qualities need to be in place before the rite is celebrated. For example, before the Rite of Acceptance into the Order of Catechumens occurs, the church must evaluate the candidates' motives and dispositions (43).[2] In particular, the Rite of Election calls for the Church to discern whether there are signs in the catechumen that God has indeed elected or chosen him or her (122). The Church is given the responsibility. Afterward, this discernment of God's action is publicly acknowledged through the testimony of the sponsors/godparents during the Rite of Election (and/or the Rite of Sending for Election). In order to give this testimony, the Church must have discerned. This Rite of Election presupposes that discernment is happening.

Discernment, then, is part of who we are as disciples, and implicitly an essential aspect of forming other disciples. Only after understanding what discernment is and how to do it can we see how it is part of the initiation process.

## For Reflection

In what ways do you sense yourself to be a discerning disciple?

Are you aware of a time when you had to choose between two good options and how you came to clarity?

What is your understanding of the role of discernment in initiation ministry?

# Chapter 2

# The Discernment Process

We have been talking about discernment without really defining it. What is this discernment that must be an ongoing part of the lives of disciples? The word comes from the Latin *discernere,* and has a sense of sifting through or separating apart. In discernment we are sifting through and separating out various feelings, beliefs, values, and inner voices in order to listen for and to the voice of the Spirit of God. Spiritual writings speak of discernment as a discernment of spirits, which is also a gift of the Spirit recognized in the early Church (1 Corinthians 12:10).

## Noticing What Spirits Are Operating

Discernment involves listening for and naming the various spirits that are operating. We listen for which spirits lead us to God and life, and which lead us away from God. We are not only looking at externals such as behavior and circumstances, though these are significant. We are also looking at what spirits are operating within us that are underneath our behavior. We have to honestly reflect on all the parts inside, such as thoughts, feelings, beliefs, and hopes, and sift through them until the truth becomes clear. For example, if I find myself always arriving late at meetings, something is going on inside that causes the behavior. Maybe I'm late because I am trying to do too much and am just packing in one more thing before I leave my house. Perhaps I'm bored at the meetings and think they are unimportant or not run well. Maybe I'm really afraid of getting more involved and making a deeper commitment.

Let's take a look at this last example. What is it about making this commitment that frightens me? Perhaps it's because I feel insecure. If I do, how might I pray about this? What else do I know about how this feeling of insecurity operates in my life? Might God want to heal this broken part in me? What is the wholeness God wants for me? Am I willing to take this broken part of myself to God in prayer?

As the above example indicates, the process of discernment begins with a noticing of what is happening in my life. Then, there is a listening within to find out what is underneath this behavior, to discover the various feelings that may be operating. In doing this, what I need to pay attention to and pray with becomes clear.

As God gives us the ability to see the truth, God also opens up the next step. Often, in naming what is going on inside, some of the fear or power of what holds us back dissipates. Then we are able to take a step forward.

## Discernment Differs from Decision-Making

Discernment is a different process from decision-making. In the latter, we often look at all the pros and cons, at possible outcomes. We may pray that God will help us make a good decision. Ultimately, we use our best judgment to make it. Ordinarily this judgment is primarily rational. But, sometimes we talk about going with a gut response. We have an instinct inside, a place of inner knowing, that feels true and is of God. This inner knowing is the place out of which discernment occurs. Discernment involves the heart, feelings, and gut instincts as well as what the mind knows.

## Discernment: Listening for God's Way

In discernment we look at the truth of our lives, of the spirits operating, and let God reveal which way truly leads to life. After naming all that is there, discernment involves holding it all before

God and saying, "What do you want for me in this situation, God?" Discernment requires listening with openness and freedom for God's desire for us, rather than a choice we make. It sifts through all that is within, holds it all before God, and listens for where God invites or leads. Discernment is a process that takes time. Its focus is on God and God's invitation. How we understand and engage in discernment will depend on our image of God and understanding of God's will, as well as aspects of self-knowledge and beliefs about feelings.

## Image of God

Now let's look at who God is for us. Since in discernment we want to listen to where God is leading, it matters who God is for us. If God is harsh, or always expecting us to do what is difficult or against our liking, then we hardly care to discern what God wants for us. Giving this God rule over our lives would be distasteful and quite risky. Discernment is grounded in an understanding of God as being a loving God—a God, as Isaiah 43 describes, who created and formed us, who tells us we are precious and loved. This is the God who communicates that we are chosen and beloved, much as Jesus experienced at his baptism.

Many people have become aware of their images of God. They will talk of their earlier sense of God as the white-bearded man keeping track of their rights and wrongs, of a perhaps kind but still judging God. Then they speak of their experience now of God as a friend, as a companion, as loving. Many will talk of an experience of a mother God, or of a creator God who simply is. Whatever the image, many people speak of their sense of a loving God.

Unfortunately, this belief in a loving God is often more at the intellectual level than an internalized experience. Asking the next question, "Do we trust God?" often gets more at the heart of the matter. Some would say, "I trust God as long as I'm in control." We might even look at what ways we are able to trust God, and where we want to maintain control. The image I connect with discernment is that of opening our hands and holding an open palm to look at what is there, and to see what it is that is of God.

In discernment we are assuming that God is loving, that what God wants for us will truly bring us happiness, and that this God wants to act in our lives. God is just waiting for the opportunity, for an opening. It is not as if we have to do something to get God to respond. God is there and ready, not wanting to impose, just desiring this involvement in our lives.

## Will of God

In more traditional language what we are trying to do is discern the will of God for us. We keep asking the question, "What does God want me to do?" "If I only knew, I'd do it." The sense here is that God's will is somewhere out there, external to ourselves, and we have to try to find out what it is. Scripture tells us it "is not too wondrous or remote. . . . No, it is something very near to you, already in your mouths and in your heart, to do it" (Deuteronomy 30:11–14).

God's will for us may not be a static or concrete thing. It might be helpful in reflecting about the meaning of God's will to think about our will for a friend. What do we want for our friends? We want them to be freely who they are, to be fully alive, to live their lives making choices that will bring about good for themselves and for others. We usually don't have specific plans for their lives. We want to honor their feelings. We want them to follow their hearts. The sense of God's will changes when we think of that will in the context of a loving God, a God who loves us even more than we love a friend.

Another way to approach the sense of God's will for us is to substitute the word *dream* for *will*. What is the quality we sense when reflecting on God's dream for us, rather than God's will? It's alive. It's in relationship. It's by someone who cares about us, knows us, and loves us. It has the sense of bringing us into the picture, who we are with our personality, talents, history, limitations, hopes, dreams, struggles, and our heart. In this discernment process of sifting through the spirits, we discover who we most are and what will bring about our true happiness, God's dream for us.

## Seeing Ourselves

Opening our hand to see what is of God also involves letting ourselves see what is there in us. We may find things we would rather not, as well as qualities that we like. This opening up process can be difficult when we discover parts of ourselves we do not like admitting to ourselves, much less to God. Often we find feelings —pain, hurt, or fear—which we would rather keep covered over or avoid. Sometimes we find behaviors, beliefs, or attitudes that we don't like acknowledging. We all have our protective layers, our defenses. In discernment we are gradually invited by a loving God to open our hands and hearts to see and feel and acknowledge our truth.

## Feelings

The area of feelings is an often difficult and important part of our spiritual lives. Feelings give us clues to what is truly going on inside us at a given time. Why are feelings difficult? Because often they are painful, messy, and an area where we feel out of control. They simply come, and we are not able to stop them. We may ignore or suppress them, but they are there. We are never taught how to work with our feelings. In school we learn how to read and write and perhaps think. Regarding feelings, we are usually taught socially acceptable ways of expressing or masking our feelings. Christian mores are often placed on top of this. For example, many people feel that they are bad if they are angry about something. They pray that God will take the anger away. We are not taught how to see that if we are angry, there may be another level of feeling underneath. Perhaps something in us or in others has been violated. The anger may be a sign or indicator that something else is out of kilter. What would it be like to journal with the anger to find out more about it? It may have to do with this isolated event. Possibly it is linked with other parts of our lives. What would it be like to see what the energy of anger is moving us toward? The anger may be an indication that we no longer fit in a particular job or situation. What would it be like to change the prayer to something such as "God, show me what you want me to see about this anger. Help me find ways to neither deny it or let it hurt others"?

Feelings are important in the spiritual life. Ignatius and other spiritual writers believe that emotions are one of the primary places where God's Spirit moves us.[2] Though conversion happens through all the parts of our being, change seldom happens without our hearts being moved. We hear people using expressions such as "My heart isn't in it," or "I already knew all the things this speaker said; what was different was that she spoke to me, to my heart—it was wonderful!" We hear the disciples who were with Jesus on the road to Emmaus reflecting on their feelings, say, "Were not our hearts burning [within us] while he spoke to us on the way and opened the scriptures to us" (Luke 24:32)? The disciples' burning hearts were indications for them of Jesus' presence.

The first step is to notice what feelings arise as we pray and live. *Do I feel afraid? Do I feel drawn to something? Am I experiencing an absence of feeling?* Then we must pay attention to whatever we notice. Paying attention to our feelings involves noticing and acknowledging them, letting ourselves feel them, telling God how we feel, and inviting God to guide us through them. In the process of letting ourselves feel our feelings, often some way of expressing them is helpful. We may want to write in a journal. This helps us acknowledge and learn more about the feelings. It gets us out of letting them go around and around inside. We may need to physically express strong feelings such as anger through voice or various physical exercises. We may need to throw something or shout in a safe private place. As we pay attention to our feelings and let ourselves feel them, they are able to shift and move.

## Resistance

We often resist letting ourselves feel the feelings that are inside. We are afraid of them. If we have held them in for a long time they may feel overwhelming and too powerful for us. We may have a sense from deep within that to acknowledge our real feelings will cause us to change something in our lives. If we are not ready to do that, we resist acknowledging our feelings.

Resistance to paying attention to our true feelings and our true selves and to taking our true selves to God in prayer is an ongoing part of the spiritual journey that we all experience. Resistance indicates that there is some movement that wants to happen. Resistance is a friend to our old selves that are comfortable with the way we are presently living. It is a protection from what is fearful or uncomfortable. When we begin to notice that we are resisting part of our true selves and our true relationship with God, then we find that we are no longer satisfied with the way things are. Something within us is propelling us forward. But at the same time we may feel stuck, unable to move. We know this is not where we want to be, but we feel unable to change. In fact, we usually do not even know how to go about changing.

It is helpful to name what the resistance feels like, to describe it, perhaps with a symbol, and to bring the resistance to prayer. For example, some say, "I feel like there's a wall around me. It's really thick, but it's beginning to crumble. Some bricks have fallen down." Then we can tell God about the resistance, and ask God for what we desire. We might pray, "God, I feel so stuck. I don't like being walled in anymore. Yet, I feel afraid of what's outside the wall. I feel vulnerable. But I do want the wall to come down. Just gently, please. I ask you to show me the way, and to be with me and give me the strength and courage to continue."

How does resistance manifest itself? It takes many forms. Sometimes we stay busy so that we do not have to feel loneliness, hurt, anxiety, or emptiness. We may work hard, read many novels, or watch a lot of television as a way of avoiding our true selves. We may eat or drink or use other drugs to keep us from feeling what's inside. We may shop or go to a mall often. We may rationalize or analyze our feelings rather than letting ourselves feel them. We may tell ourselves, "I shouldn't feel this way" or "I'll only feel worse if I let myself feel the pain inside." We may walk around wearing a mask, acting like everything is ok, wearing a big smile. We may be focused on others and taking care of their needs to keep us from noticing our own. Perhaps you can add to this list. We all have our own patterns of resistance.

Moving through resistance may take time, even months. Yet, when we come out the other side we find we are living at a deeper, more satisfying level. Understanding resistance at a rational level is helpful, but it is not a rational process. It occurs within our emotions and our whole being. Working with resistance can be difficult. It is helpful to know that resistance is part of the spiritual journey and that we are not "bad" or doing something wrong when we experience it. Companions can be helpful in lending support and compassion as we work with our resistance.

## Inner Voices

As we continue to pay attention to our inner spirits, we also begin to notice little voices or tapes within ourselves—almost as if we have a radio playing in our heads. Somewhat constant processing and "self-talk" goes on inside. When we begin to pay closer attention we find patterns there. Each of us has this, but the patterns are different from one person to another. We might always be telling ourselves we are stupid, not very attractive, not as organized as others, unimportant, or always the loser. On the other hand, we might be very critical of others and blame ourselves for this. Generally, if we are hard on others we are even harder on ourselves. We start to identify the spirits operating when we notice and bring this self-talk to consciousness. Noticing our self-talk is a step toward naming our own areas of unfreedom. Once this occurs, we are able to journal, pray, and reflect on these areas within ourselves.

For those of us working with the initiation process, it is important to name our inner tapes and look at them not only for our personal wholeness, but also to be able to be free to discern with others on their journeys. If candidates or catechumens do not fit the idealized version we have, we will not be free to really listen to their experience and to walk with them where God leads. For example, we may find something about the person's manner of dress or appearance not fitting our standards and be unconsciously judging him or her. When someone is repeatedly late for the Liturgy of the Word or a catechumenate session, our beliefs about tardiness may lead to strong negative feelings or judgments that prevent us from listening to what is really happening within the person's life around the issue. We may hear about a woman having had an abortion or someone having had an affair. It is possible that our strong feelings about such experiences could keep us from listening to the person. Our own expectations or biases will affect how we see and hear others' lives and journeys. To be able to discern with others, it is absolutely necessary to come to know our own inner messages.

Other voices we carry within ourselves are the "shoulds," often messages from authorities that we have internalized: *You should always work hard. You should keep your problems to yourself. You should always be neat and clean. You shouldn't cry in public. You should keep your feelings to yourself. You shouldn't make waves. You should always be polite ...* Each of us reading this can think of many more "shoulds," or the particular ones ingrained in ourselves. They have become automatic rules of life that may or may not fit who we are and what we really believe. They may make us self-critical and other-critical because no one could ever measure up to all of them. The discernment process invites us to bring to consciousness and examine these different "tapes," so that we are not ruled by them and can freely make choices.

## Desire

Desire is also an important aspect of discernment, because often through desire God invites and moves us. I am not talking about the desire to win the lottery or to get a more expensive house. I am speaking of the desire we have in our inner selves, in our hearts, and in our relationship with God. We might desire to find ways of living more out of our own truth rather than of pleasing everyone else. We might want to be able to bring our fear and anxiety to God in prayer rather than ignoring our feelings. We might desire to open our hands to God more and let God take the lead in our lives.

Many of us feel selfish giving attention to a spiritual desire we have. We do not realize that this desire is placed in us by God. We are generally very comfortable praying for the needs of others, but would never think of bringing our own needs to God. We might pray "to do God's will," a good prayer, though quite general. We are simply not used to paying attention to what we desire. Jesus invited the two disciples following him to name their desire with the question, "What are you looking for?" They did not answer the question, but responded with a slight change of topic, "Where are you staying?" (John 1:38). They avoided naming the real desire in their hearts, which may have been something such as "There's something special about you. We'd like to get to know you better."

At times we desire something from God, but other desires exist in us as well. We want a closer relationship with God, but we also want to stay in control. We want to do what God wants, but we don't want to change anything in our lives. What if God asks us to give up a relationship or a job that we know is unhealthy, or to deal with a problem area of life? Fear of what God wants may be a barrier to praying for what we desire. We know the story of the rich man who asked Jesus what he must do for everlasting life (Mark 10:17–22). He really wanted to live more deeply with God. Yet, he was not ready to do what was required. His desire for the fullness of life was there, but other parts of him at this moment were stronger. We do not know what happened to him after this encounter. He may have just let go of his desire to live more closely with God. Or, over time, he may have prayed with his feelings and resistances until his desire became stronger and he could let go of what held him back from what his heart wanted.

If God plants the desire in our hearts, then perhaps God is waiting for us to pray that desire so that God can respond to it and we can move closer to God. The image I have is of God reeling us in closer and closer with a fishing rod. God places the desires of the Spirit within us, and then waits for us to "bite," to bring those desires to consciousness and prayer. God always gives us space and waits for our response before reeling us in a little closer. God has utter respect for us and our timing, is patient, and even gives us the freedom to stay at a safe distance. Praying our desire brings us into closer, personal relationship with God. Although risky, praying our desire makes us vulnerable to God, and often leads to more letting go of control to God, and it usually opens us to deeper life.

## Opening to Ourselves and to God

Opening up our hands and ourselves, then, means that we might have to let things unfold differently than we would initially want. As if we could control them anyway! Opening up feels risky and takes courage and trust. As we open, we find that our trust relationship with God deepens, our relationship with ourselves grows, and it becomes easier and easier to open further. This is the ongoing path of discernment to which we are invited.

Being discerning persons, then, invites us to live our lives in deep honesty. We grow in freedom as we can let ourselves see and feel what is inside. And we end up trusting God more and more in the process. We let God be more and more involved in our lives. This inner movement to truth and freedom and deeper connection with God is exhibited in the Samaritan woman. The amazing statement she makes after her encounter with Jesus is to come and see someone who told her everything she ever did (John 4:29). Most of us would not be pleased about someone knowing everything we ever did. We would want to cover ourselves and hide, as did Adam and Eve in their naked-ness. So, why is the Samaritan woman proclaiming this to the whole town? Because she was freed inside. The truth of her life was revealed, and she was accepted and loved. This freedom and acceptance were cause for great rejoicing. Through paying atten-tion, discerning, and gradually opening more to God, this same deep freedom and joy are available to us. We must do our part, and God will always be ready to meet us and do much more than what we ask or imagine (Ephesians 3:20).

Becoming or living as discerning persons is a process, a way of life. We do not just decide to sit down for the next forty-five minutes and discern something. It takes time, possibly weeks or months. It requires an ongoing attention to our inner spirits, a noticing of the different voices, feelings, impulses, resistances, desires. Discernment, then, involves the process of opening our hands to see, feel, appreciate what is there and to sift through it. Discernment takes place in relationship with God, in a context of prayer, asking God to be the one to reveal in this area what is moving us toward God and God's Spirit, and what is moving us away. Discernment involves our opening of ourselves to our truth and to God's dream for us.

As we sit in prayer and reflection and sift through all that is inside, additional time may be needed to act on what we hear.

Sometimes we see or know the truth and what must be done before we are ready inside to live it. More time is needed for our inner selves to be ready to live what is being heard inside. And at other times our inner selves are ready to move, to live out what is discerned. Just paying attention to all that is within—feeling feelings, naming voices, and attending—often gives clarity and freedom to our inner spirits. The movement simply happens.

The discernment process is about paying attention to all that is inside, for this is the material of the spirits we must sift through. An inherent belief that God's Spirit lives within us is operative. As we deeply pay attention, sift through, listen, notice, and see in freedom, we come in touch with more than our own spirits. We come in touch with that place where the Spirit of God dwells.

Discernment leads us to be able to see which spirits are operating and which are of God so that we may choose to live in God's dream for us.

## Support of Other Disciples

Being discerning disciples is an invitation to live our lives fully and deeply with God. Living as discerning disciples affects who we are and all of our relationships. The processes just described are not always easy. So it is important to keep in mind that disciples are not individuals on a journey, but are part of a Church of disciples. We need others who are also on their journeys to this deeper way of living. Knowing that others are taking their journeys seriously encourages us to do the same. We also need one another to help us listen to ourselves. Often we are blind to the movements within until we have another person help us sift through them. We are so close to what is within that we need others who are outside ourselves to help us clarify and name the spirits that operate.

Living this path of discernment is a prerequisite for the Church, and in particular the initiation team, if we are to discern with those who come for initiation. We cannot discern with them in their lives unless we are familiar with that process within ourselves. Only by living and working with discernment in our own lives do we come to understand it. This understanding, knowing from experience, is what best gives us what we need both to discern with others and to hand the process of discernment on to them.

### For Reflection

What are some of the patterns of self-talk that you are aware of within yourself? How do they affect you?

What are three of your most frequent feelings? What do you generally do with them? At times, what are the ways you resist your feelings?

Is asking God for what you want unusual or comfortable for you? Are you able to name what you desire? How would it feel to take this desire to prayer?

Describe the process of how you discerned about something in your own life. Name the issues, feelings involved, desire, and shifts as you prayed with this concern.

# Chapter 3
# The Way of Discerning Listening

Discerning with others along the way in the initiation process
will include various kinds of listening moments with them.
Discerning listening is necessary as a part of the discernment
process before the celebration of specific rites. Throughout the
initiation process sponsors and other initiation ministers also
will be part of one-on-one listening moments with the person.
We now turn our attention to exploring this type of individual
listening, what it is, how to do it, and its value.

## The Gift of Being Listened To

On a basic day-to-day level, having someone listen to us is
a unique gift. More often, our experience is that when we tell
another something, the response is often quick and the conversation moves on to something else. At times an extraneous detail
may be highlighted rather than the real experience. For example:

"I just got back from Lourdes."

"What was the weather like over there?"

Or perhaps when we state something that just happened
to us, the listener responds with information, or with another
personal experience. As an example, I recently shared an experience that when driving to a meeting my car skidded, slid out
of control, and I was almost hit broadside. Rather than anyone
asking what that was like for me, I was questioned as to exactly
what I did and told how to maneuver a car when it slides. I also
remember that when my mother was dying someone told me,
"I know this is hard, but I'm sure you know she'll be better off

when she dies." These were not my feelings at the time! Each of us is able to name experiences from simple or important moments of our lives when someone failed to listen to us.

## Listening Helps When Living a Busy Lifestyle

We are all busy, and often just keep on going without a lot of attention to what is happening within us. Or, at times, our feelings are so strong or we feel so confused or afraid of them that we keep busy to avoid what is really happening inside. We often need someone to listen to us to help us get to the deeper part of ourselves. When someone is listening, we first spend time talking about many aspects of our present lives. It is only after this layer of content gets named that we can go to a deeper level. In such a busy and fast-paced culture, having someone listen to us helps provide the space to notice our inner experience and feelings. The listening presence of another provides a helpful support in attending to our inner journey.

## Discerning Listening

Being a listening presence is a way of assisting others to hear God within them. Our own experiences are so close to us that we cannot see or name them clearly. We truly need someone else to listen with us to see and hear the different spirits operating within ourselves. This kind of listening to those in the initiation process to help them sift through spirits inside is a way that the coordinator and various initiation ministers often will be present to them. It is different from being a friend and doing faith sharing, or mutual sharing of each other's journey. This process involves a conscious focus on one person's journey. It is a giving over of ourselves to be a listening presence to that person. This one-on-one listening experience begins with the first meeting the coordinator of initiation has with the inquirer, and occurs periodically throughout the process.

## Trusting God's Spirit Within Us

Listening with another for how God is present and acting in his or her life takes seriously the scripture and belief that by Baptism we are made temples of the Holy Spirit (1 Corinthians 3:16). The Holy Spirit really dwells within the person we are accompanying. A great gift we can offer is to be a listening presence to the Spirit's action within the other. As listening companions we put aside our own journeys for the moment, our ideas and insights, and become present to what is happening in the other. If the Holy Spirit dwells within the person, then his or her feelings, needs, and desires are good. The resources for any next steps and decisions ahead lie within that person. This belief that answers and resources lie within the person, rather than with the advice or suggestion another offers, is essential if we choose to be discerning listeners.

This listening also takes the Incarnation seriously. God took on human flesh in Jesus and continues to do so today. God is alive in the flesh of people, and acts within the real life of the person, within his or her thoughts, needs, feelings, desires, and experiences. God does not just speak through things that are traditionally thought of as "holy," but through all of life. Everything becomes sacred and an arena for God's action—grace. So the focus of discerning listening is what is most important to the person, where the real experience and energy of the person's life are. This may include areas like getting or losing a job, having a baby, sexuality, getting married or divorced, social, political, or justice concerns, a conflict within the family, illness, and so on. Real human life is where God dwells and acts. We need not be talking only about prayer or specifically "religious" events to be doing true discerning listening, though these areas are obviously not excluded. We are listening with another for where real-life experience intersects with God experience.

## Listening Skills

Discerning listening uses simple skills that may feel awkward at first. With practice they become natural. What follows is a naming and some examples of these listening skills.[1]

### Giving Reflective Feedback

A listener may reflect the meaning, content, and especially the feeling heard by paraphrasing, using a sentence, or repeating a phrase or word in a simple and brief way. Responses that include the effect give evidence to hearing the person at a deeper level than the facts that have been shared. The following examples include an acknowledgment of the feeling the person has conveyed:

- "It sounds as if these last two weeks have been very difficult for you."

- "You seem really angry."

- "Deeply tired."

- "What your friend said has left you feeling hurt and confused."

- "Your new job seems to symbolize this new you, a you with confidence and energy."

- "Very frustrated."

- "I see the tears in your eyes as you speak about this."

Try this kind of response and notice the effect. People will really take in and own what they have said. They will hear their own experience in a new and deeper way through your simple words. At times they will say, "You're right. I didn't realize how tired, angry, alive, scared I am." At other times they will go on to say more about what they are experiencing. It is as if what has been said, especially noting the feelings, gives them a sense of trust in you. You have heard them. And your statement shows you are really listening to them, a gift that isn't often given. People then feel that they can trust you and are freed to say more about their experience. Just having the opportunity to express what is inside is beneficial for people.

### Inviting a Further Exploration

Another skill that is helpful in assisting others to touch deeply into their truth is to ask them to expand on what they've just said. For example:

- "Can you say more about the fear that you're feeling?"

- "What's it like for you as you sit with your dying mother?"

- "How does it feel to have so many questions inside?"

- "Do you have an image for how that hurt feels?"

- "You're touching your heart. What are you feeling there?"

In an initial interview for someone interested in becoming part of the Catholic Church, we might ask:

- "Can you say more about what it was like for you growing up as a Baptist?"

- "Are you able to put into words what it is you're looking for?"

- "How does it feel for you as you think of beginning this journey with us?"

We would avoid the following questions: "Why do you feel that way?" "And then what did you do?" "Who else was there with you?" "What would God say?" All of these questions lead persons away from their experience and usually cause people to analyze, to go into their heads to figure out a response. Other questions are simply informational and put us, the listeners, in the lead as to where the conversation goes next. Rather, we are there to simply enable others to articulate their faith journeys.

## Summarizing

At times, we might reflect back the bigger picture we are hearing by giving summarizing statements or asking a clarifying question for the focus of the conversation. For example:

"So, your wife and son go up to Communion every week and you feel separated from them as you sit in the pew. But you also sense something in them, in their relationship with God, that you'd like to have." This summary lets the person know you understand what is being said, and enables him or her to move on and share more of the experience.

"You talked about the delight you feel with your two children as they are growing up, and how happy you are with choices you've made for yourself. This seems to be a very positive and hopeful time in your life." Our putting together of these different aspects helps the person see the bigger picture of what's happening in his or her life.

"You are concerned both about getting a job and about your relationship with your friend, John. Is there one of these you'd like to spend more time talking about?" This question allows the person to focus and to choose the direction of the conversation.

These may feel like techniques at first. After we use them for awhile, we will find our own styles and words that feel natural.

# Listening Pitfalls

It is not just the unnaturalness or unfamiliarity with these skills that keep discerning listeners from truly attending to the other's journey. All listeners generally experience personal difficulties in this type of listening. It is helpful to know our own styles and the, perhaps, unconscious things we say and do which get in the way of our truly listening to another. Following are examples of common tendencies discerning listeners might have that are neither helpful nor listening.

### Advice-giving

Many people who listen to others are in the habit of giving advice:

- "I think you should . . ."
- "Why don't you . . ."
- "If I were you, I'd . . ."
- "I'd suggest you . . ."
- "When I was in a situation like that, I . . ."

What's wrong with giving advice? It is not discerning listening. The listening presence that truly believes the Holy Spirit dwells within the person and will give the needed insights and resources does not happen when advice is given. In fact, the opposite occurs. Giving advice takes the person away from listening within where God speaks and moves him or her to find the answer "out there," through another authority, you. As listeners we must be aware of our own needs and feelings as we listen with another who is waiting to know an answer or path. Listeners who give advice often fill their own needs to fix things up, to rescue another, to get away from the discomfort of not knowing what to do. Perhaps such listeners are not at ease by allowing the person to feel uncomfortable feelings without having them resolved. Giving advice also may make the listeners feel good simply to have had an answer, a solution. How awesome if we choose to be responsible for another's path. Just because something has worked for us, it will not necessarily work for another. No matter how similar, another person and situation are different. Each person needs to find his or her own solutions.

It is true that at times people ask advice of discerning listeners. "They want to know what I think or what I'd suggest." Yes, they do—and no, they do not. Yes, they do because it seems easier to get an answer from someone rather than engaging in their own searching process. No, they do not because they really do want to find their own way. Notice how often advice will be readily received, but rarely acted upon. More often you'll hear "I know you said I should . . . , but I didn't do that. Instead, I . . . "

Is there ever a place for offering suggestions or advice-giving with inquirers and catechumens? Yes, of course. At times, suggestions may be very appropriate. Those such as "Why don't you try the precatechumenate for a month and see where you are then?" or "You may want to talk with your spouse and children separately and together about your concerns" give the inquirer or catechumen an approach to take. However, the initiation minister who is listening needs to separate when he or she is there as a listener to attend to the other, and facilitate the person finding the answer within, from offering specific options about the Church or a part of the initiation process. Any one conference could involve both of these moments. Since most of us have a tendency to err on the side of offering advice rather than assisting the other in finding his or her own way, I would caution the listener to be careful and attentive in the area of giving advice.

## Avoiding Pain and Painful Feelings

"You're feeling down, but you have so many gifts and strengths. Why don't you focus on them. Let's name your strengths." Or, "Let me give you a hug. Why don't you go home, make yourself a cup of hot tea, and get some rest. You'll feel better tomorrow." This is another pitfall of a discerning listener and, again, comes out of the listener's need to help the other feel better. Trying to cover the pain does not take it away. Focusing on strengths or gifts is not what the other person needs. It's a temporary awareness that will not last for long. What is most helpful is for the person to really explore the painful feelings with the presence and support of another. An exception is when a person has a very negative self-image. Dwelling with this pain will only lead such a person further into a pit.

Listeners who always want the other to feel good may want to get in touch with what they do with their own painful feelings. Do they cover them up with busyness, work, TV, or food? Do they avoid feeling their own pain? Do they believe it is more valuable to be happy than to go through the inner journey of being real, and letting true happiness come out of this process and relationship with God?

## Spiritualizing, Especially with Clichés

- "God will take care of you."
- "Just keep praying and trust."
- "God never sends more than you can handle."
- "God must have a reason that you'll know someday."
- "Just offer it up."
- "God knows what's best."

You can add others to the list above. What's wrong with these statements? Again, the listener is telling the person how to think or what to do. These bromides are ways we have of coping with painful situations. They keep us from expressing our real hurt, and at times, anger to God. They address our minds, not our feelings. They keep us from trusting, again, that God truly lives in and through our human lives—our real, messy human lives. We need not reason away the pain, but rather express what is truly there to God in prayer. For example, if a listener tells the person simply to trust, he or she may feel uneasy about feeling any fear involved: "I know I shouldn't be afraid. If I really trusted God I wouldn't be afraid." Is it possible to trust God and to also feel afraid? Fear is a feeling. Trust and fear may both be there. God is bigger than we are and is able to handle our real feelings, even anger. In fact, in being real with God about our feelings, we open up a true place in ourselves for deeper relationship with God. The words *should* or *try* are usually a clue that a person has left who he or she really is to be some ideal that is not true at the moment. It is difficult for humans to believe that God came for us as we are. It is important for listeners not to reinforce this idealizing by using these spiritual clichés, but rather to value what is real within the person.

## Giving Suggestions from Our Own Lives

"I know how you feel. My mother died two years ago." We really do not know how another feels. Another's relationship with his or her mother is different from ours. Instead we might ask, "What was it like for you as you sat with your mother while she was dying?" The response will vary, depending on what the relationship between the mother and person had been.

Listeners might also insert a personal experience into the conversation: "When I used this Scripture passage of the Annunciation you're talking about, I recalled all the angels who have come into my own life." Though an experience is very meaningful for us, it may not be for the other person. This sharing has put the focus on our own lives, and has taken it off the experience of the person to whom we are listening. At times the person will believe we are the ones with the right understanding, and will put his or her own experience aside. Perhaps with this Scripture the person has been taken with the sense of being called by God, of Mary's faithfulness, or of all the change this will entail for her. But we may never hear about this if we state our meaning first. Another way listeners move into our own journeys is by a phrase such as "I've had that experience, too. Here's what I do." Again, the focus moves to the listener.

## Acknowledging Our Biases

As discerning listeners, we need to be aware of the places inside where we are not free. Are there any people about whom we have such strong feelings or judgments that we would not be able to be truly present to them and their life and concerns? For example, it is important that we know how we feel about someone who is in a second or third marriage, who is gay or lesbian, who has had an abortion, who is living on welfare, who is a feminist, who is of a different racial heritage, who smokes, or who has a fundamentalist approach to Scripture. Or perhaps there is a quality about someone's personality that is very off-putting to us. The person may seem overbearing, or too mousy. We could feel afraid of this kind of man or woman. Or we may have this person so much on a pedestal, that we cannot hear his or her real person and limitations. If I have strong feelings about the person, I am probably not free simply to listen. We will most always have another agenda of changing or chiding the person in some way.

## Knowing Ourselves as Listeners

We must each get to know ourselves, our own styles, our kinds of words and expressions, and the effects they have on where and how deep the conversation goes. Listeners may ask for honest feedback: "Out of our conversation today, what has been most helpful for you? Did anything I said feel jolting or out of sync with where you are? I'd really like you to answer honestly." Giving over our attention to the other involves true self-gift, and a putting aside of our own need for attention, to rescue, to give advice, to share. Though these skills can be learned, some initiation ministers may find they have natural gifts in this area. Others may discover that their natural preferences are not in this deeper listening, and they may want to be engaged in other aspects of the initiation process that more readily use their gifts.

## Qualities of Discerning Listeners

Various attributes characterize those who listen well to others. These same qualities assist the listener in his or her own personal development. The old adage "we learn by doing" is true. We are not able to do for others what we do not do in our own lives. To truly be able to listen to another requires that we first are willing to be present to our real self. I think of the truism of the directions to parents regarding the use of the oxygen mask on the plane: "Put your own oxygen mask on first, and then put one on your child." We cannot truly serve others with a listening presence if we are unwilling to do this for ourselves.

## Self-aware

Initiation ministers who have the listening conversations with inquirers, catechumens, and candidates need to be aware of what is happening within themselves as they listen. In listening to others, one is continually making choices of what to say or not say: Do I interject here, summarize, or let the person unfold more before I speak? Do I go back to the feeling the person was just expressing, or focus on where the conversation is now? The listener is using intuition, and one's own sense of what may be helpful to the other to make the choice. But, in deciding what might be a helpful response, the listener must be aware of why he or she would choose one statement over another.

Those who listen to others are not perfect in this. Perfection is not the goal. Rather, the willingness to keep devoting time and energy to the inner journey is necessary. Discerning listeners are engaged with their own feelings. Some do this in quiet reflection. Others find it helpful to journal about their feelings. If one has not given attention to one's own feelings, they come out in how one lives, and affect how one listens to another. For example, in reflecting on her experience of listening, one woman told me she found it hard to listen to another woman who seemed "helpless." When we explored how "helplessness" was part of her own life, she realized that she does not like herself when she feels helpless. She has always avoided this feeling, and has continually tried to "pull herself up by her own bootstraps." She then gave some time to reflecting and journaling on her experience of helplessness within herself. In a more recent conversation, she found she was able to listen to a woman who also was feeling helpless.

### Are Listened To

Often it is said that experience is the best teacher. Effective listeners usually know the experience of sharing their thoughts and feelings with another. Thus, the person knows what it is like to be vulnerable with another, to open oneself on progressively deeper levels, to choose to share or not share dimensions of one's heart. Through the experience of revealing oneself to another in this way, one who will be the listener will learn to be more and more compassionate and accepting.

### Enjoy Communicative Relationships

Generally, those who are effective listeners enjoy people and relate easily with them. Listeners are trustworthy, and are often sought out by others for their "listening ear." Good listeners appreciate being present to another and his or her life. They are comfortable with the "stuff" of human experience, including tears and the broad range of feelings. In their own relationships, listeners share who they are, how they feel, and engage in honest responses.

### Listen to God

Besides listening to themselves and to others, effective listeners know how to listen inwardly to God. They are willing to follow what they hear from God, even if to do so is challenging. Their prayer often involves some quiet reflection, as well as speaking their feelings, needs, and desires to God. They are familiar with the process of waiting, of sifting through their thoughts and feelings, of sensing the truth of others in a given situation, and of opening to God's direction.

## Listening Is Redemptive

Why is this kind of listening important? Each of us has an ideal self that judges the real self, particularly in the area of feelings. The ideal self tells us we shouldn't be angry, we should love everyone, we should be understanding, patient, and so on. However, these

feelings of anger, impatience, sadness, or hurt are real. Often
a person with strong feelings feels confused, like everything is
jumbled. Listening helps one identify all the feelings and values
involved, and in doing this, find clarity. The listening process
helps a person know that he or she is truly good. Listening is a
supportive action to enable the person to look within, to accept
what is there, and to make choices. Researchers have found that
people who have come to a deeper sense of themselves, and of
their own inner authority and voice, can almost always cite
a significant person who truly listened to them and took what they
said seriously, someone who gave his or her focus and attention to
them, and found their feelings and experience important.[2]

Listening with another and being listened to is an
experience of intimacy. A person is being believed in, accepted,
and trusted. Listening brings about a connection, from a feeling
of aloneness and alienation, to a feeling of belonging. In all of
these ways, the listening process brings about the experience of
liberation. Listening is part of the redemptive liberating work
of Christ.

## Listening Skills Assist in Various Ministries

In some degree, listening skills are useful and valuable not only
in a one-on-one situation, but in the various roles assumed by
initiation ministers. You may sense ways these skills could be
used in leading precatechumenate sessions. Catechists in each of
the stages of the initiation process are also interactive as they lead
sessions. The skills that were just discussed can help catechists take
the sessions they lead to a deeper level.

In many of the conferences with inquirers, catechumens,
and candidates we will assume more than one role. At times
we will need to provide information, respond to questions, invite
a stating of concerns, or challenge and state our expectations.
Sponsors, too, need to move back and forth between being listeners and sharing their own faith. We each need to be clear in

ourselves about when we are in one role or another, even within the same encounter. This will give us a better facility of being the listening presence at the moments when this focus will be the most advantageous to the inquirer, catechumen, or candidate.

### For Reflection

Name a time when you felt really listened to by another. What was this experience like for you? What was the effect in you from this kind of listening presence?

Recall a time when you were expressing something and were not really listened to. What was this like for you?

What are your gifts as a listener? What are your difficulties? Name one new way you are willing to try listening to another.

# Chapter 4

# Discernment in the Precatechumenate

Discernment during the precatechumenate period has its own special meaning. This period runs from the time when the person makes the initial phone call inquiring about "becoming Catholic" to the Rite of Acceptance into the Order of Catechumens. The *Rite of Christian Initiation of Adults* is clear that each person should be considered individually, as having a unique faith journey. Although some may be ready, not every inquirer is automatically to participate in the Rite of Acceptance the next time it is celebrated. The RCIA tells us "to evaluate, and, if necessary, to purify the candidates' motives and dispositions" (43). It also states that "sponsors, catechists, and deacons, parish priests (pastors) have the responsibility for judging the outward indications of such dispositions" (43).

## The Initial Interview

The attitude that the inquirer is on a journey of faith and the awareness that the person comes because of God's movement comprise the context of the initial interview. Whoever usually conducts it, conveys this vision.

Often in this first interview there is great concern to get the "facts." Baptized or not? Married? Annulment needed? If the inquirer is married, is the spouse Catholic? If there are children, are they Catholic? Or have they been part of another faith tradition? While all of this is important information, we want to set up a dynamic in this first interview that would invite the person to reflect on and articulate some real-life and God experience. As a start, more open-ended questions would be helpful: "Can you say a little about what's drawing you to the Catholic Church?" Follow the inquirer's lead and invite him or her to name more about this experience. Perhaps a rather factual response will come: "My child will be receiving her first communion in May and I want to be able to receive with her and my spouse." We could take the conversation to a deeper level by asking, "Is there anything you are looking for in the Church?" or "What's been your experience of church as you've come to Mass with your spouse?" We might specifically invite the inquirer to talk about his or her relationship with God. It also would be helpful to discuss job or school, family or living situation, all part of the person's real life where God acts. Whatever the responses, we can employ some of the listening skills noted in the previous chapter. Use reflective statements or words, or ask a further open-ended question inviting the inquirer to go deeper and express more about what has been said. Of course, at the initial interview we will need to speak about this process as a faith journey, when the inquiry sessions will take place, and any other necessary details, as well as inviting questions or concerns the person has.

What's the effect of this type of interview? The person will begin to form a relationship that is deeper than ordinary. As the person shares some of his or her story with us, the seeds of a trusting relationship will be sown. The inquirer will begin to get a sense that this is not a program whose goal is simply for him or her to become Catholic. Instead, the person will bring his or her real self, real life, real questions and desires, and real relationship with God to this moment. The interview will set up in the inquirer the expectation that he or she is the active agent in the process, rather than a sense of coming each evening to see what "they're going to be talking about tonight." Also, the inquirer will begin to realize that this process will take time.

## Movements during the Precatechumenate

And so the inquirer begins the period of precatechumenate, a time of evangelization (36) and of "faith and initial conversion that cause a person to feel called away from sin and drawn into the mystery of God's love" (37). Notice the important word *feel* in the description of the conversion that is to unfold. The inquirer is not only to attend regularly the precatechumenate sessions. Much more than that is being said. Something new or deeper is to happen. The goal is more than the inquirer knowing what the Church believes about sin and God's love. Rather, the desire of the Church is that the person begins to feel this movement away from sin and into the mystery of God's love. Things start to shift inside. New perspectives and visions begin opening up.

Over the weeks, the precatechumenate ministers begin to look for and hear the inquirers talk about these movements or shifts that are happening. They listen for real flesh to be put on the meaning of the words "feel called away from sin and drawn into the mystery of God's love." They might hear this expressed in words such as "I'm finding I'm different at work. One person there really annoys me, but I'm somehow a lot more understanding toward her. It's like I now have some compassion where I used to be filled with judgment. I am able to be friendlier to her." Or another may talk about relationship with God: "I didn't think about God very much. Now I find that I talk to God like a friend. It's as if God is always there with me." Someone may talk about his or her life in relationship to family: "I wasn't a very nice person to be around. I don't know how my spouse stood me. I guess I'm just a lot happier and so I'm more pleasant." Or someone may talk about life in relationship to others: "I was definitely the center of my world. Now I would say God is. And that helps me see and notice others around me differently. I've started volunteering some of my time at the food pantry." At times, a person begins dealing with a long-term broken relationship: "My one married sister hasn't been with the rest of us on Christmas for four years—since my mother's death.

We have all been angry at her lack of caring for Mom during her illness, and the way she was at the funeral. Inside, part of me has felt bad about that, but I've just put it aside because I felt hurt. I know now that I need to call her and begin working through this separation."

## Facilitating the Movements

These statements are solid gold. When spoken, they are to be noted, dwelt on, and reverenced. This is one area where the skills of good discerning listeners are important for precatechumenate ministers. We first need to notice that what is being said is a real lived experience of what the rite is saying in the words "feel called away from sin and drawn into the mystery of God's love" (37). Then, as discerning listeners, the ministers want to stay with the experience the person has named, to let him or her know that it was heard and to facilitate its going deeper and expanding. We might give a simple reflective listening statement or phrase, or invite the person to share about how it feels to experience this shift. When a person is talking about this movement within, tears frequently appear. A simple statement like "There's a lot of emotion in you with this" helps the person stay with the feelings, and know that they are acceptable and welcome in this environment. When these feelings come up, we are in the place of the heart that is to be deeply reverenced. It is a signal that real movement is happening, and it is a place of God's sacred action.

## Need for Discernment

The language of the RCIA is that of evaluation and "responsibility for judging the outward indications of such dispositions" (43). Words of evaluation rather than the language of discernment are used. However, it is clear that it is the responsibility of the Church to make this determination. The intention is not to judge what is inside the person but rather to be attentive to ways these dispositions may be manifested. When we go to the previous paragraph (42) and see the dispositions being referred to as necessary for the celebration of the Rite of Acceptance into the Order of Catechumens, we come upon a sense of listening for the movement of God within the person, or discernment.

We are looking for outward indications of an *initial* conversion. The meaning of *conversion* from its Latin root is to turn, to change into, to transform. In other words, we are looking for a shift or movement in inquirers, in their "relationship with God in Christ" and an "intention to change their lives" (42). The RCIA further specifies what this conversion entails. The evidence being sought is that of "stirrings of repentance," "the practice of calling upon God in prayer, a sense of the Church, and some experience of the company and spirit of Christians." These are concrete ways of naming that a person is in the process of being converted, of being transformed, that the opening within the person's heart and whole being is beginning to happen. The person has moved from an initial desire to be Catholic to opening the various parts of self and life to God's action in new ways.

## Moments of Discernment

### Precatechumenate sessions

There are different moments of this discernment with the individual inquirers in the precatechumenate. One happens week by week with the precatechumenate ministers as they listen for statements the inquirers make about the shifts or conversion happening within them. These will not be in the language of the text, but in the language of real-life experience. The leaders listen and reflect back, helping the inquirer take note of this movement. They invite the inquirer to stay with the experience by using reflective phrases or invitational questions. The leaders help name this movement that God is doing within the inquirer.

## The Individual Conference

A second moment of the discernment is an individual conference with the inquirer, which could be held by the coordinator, the person who did the initial conference, or another initiation minister. The role of the person in initiation is not as important here as is who has the skill for doing the kind of listening needed. It may or may not be one of the paid professionals on the staff. Perhaps there is a trained spiritual director in the parish, or another person who has background in this kind of discerning listening. We initiation ministers must honestly talk with one another about who has these gifts and skills. The inquirers and their journeys are too important to just let anyone meet with them.

Before the conference occurs it is important to inform the inquirer that we are in a discernment process to determine when the right time will be for movement into the catechumenate. Hopefully, this sense of discernment was already communicated to the inquirer during the initial interview and will not come as a surprise. We want the inquirer to know that he or she will be asked to talk about his or her experience, and that some of us involved in initiation will be meeting in a prayerful context to discern readiness for movement into the catechumenate. We will be in dialogue with the inquirer along the way. We want to listen for the truth of how God is moving in his or her life. This discernment process should occur several weeks before the Rite of Acceptance is scheduled, so that we are not first stating the date for the celebration, setting up an expectation, and then wanting to discern. The discernment has to be made in freedom.

## Areas of Life Explored

In the individual conference we want to invite the inquirer to talk about his or her inner experience during this time of precatechumenate: how he or she is being affected in different areas of life including family or other significant relationships, sense of self, work situation, and feeling about the Catholic Church. We can use the various listening skills to help the inquirer name and articulate his or her deeper experience. We might ask explicitly about his or her relationship with God, what he or she senses is God's invitation for further growth, or what is desired from God at this time. Of course, we also need to talk about what would be asked of the inquirer should there be a readiness to move into the catechumenate, and a little about the ritual celebration itself. If sponsors have not already been discussed, we need to do so. We invite questions or concerns the person has, and any input about the experience of the precatechumenate. It is also important to get permission to relate to other team members some of what the inquirer has shared. If anything shared is confidential, we may not share it until we have permission.

### Raising Concerns

The person conducting this individual conference elicits from other initiation ministers beforehand any questions or concerns about the inquirer moving on to the catechumenate so that these can be talked about. Often, I find that in raising these issues the person acknowledges the truth of what is inside: "You're right. I'm really not into all of this now. It would be nice to be Catholic, but I'm not sure I'm ready at this time." Or, "Yes, my work has been taking all of my time, and I want to devote my energy toward that." We could invite the person to continue to come to precatechumenate sessions whenever he or she would like, and slow down the whole process a bit. Another inquirer may respond by talking a little deeper about present struggles. Or the person may be somewhat defensive. However, in talking we are honest about our concerns. Bringing them out in the open may be what is needed to help the inquirer look at something that is happening in his or her life.

In discussing something conflictual, it is helpful to give specific examples and stay away from general phrases. Once an initiation minister told me she smelled alcohol on the inquirer's breath at a morning activity. I was the lucky one to talk about this with the inquirer. I got permission to share this information, and then began in a private setting: "I have something difficult to talk with you about." Usually we are only open to acknowledging a wounded part of ourselves with another if we trust him or her and really believe that he or she cares for us. The foundation of trust and relating in real truth are necessary for such a conversation to come off well. One conversation gives a basis for another. Keep in mind this is a process, and it takes time for movement to happen in his or her life.

### Discernment Process

The third moment of the discernment is the meeting in a prayerful context of those on the team who are responsible for naming whether the outer signs of the stated dispositions are there. This might include the initiation coordinator, two or three precatechumenate ministers, and a parish priest. A local parish needs to decide who is best to be part of this meeting. One method that might be used is to take some time for prayer, of putting this discernment process in the awareness that we are listening for God's action, for movement in these people's lives. One by one either the interviewer or a precatechumenate minister may present the person and the signs of readiness noticed, or any questions or concerns. After the input is given about a specific person, the members gathered spend some time in prayer, and in listening within themselves to their sense of how God is moving within this inquirer. Then, they may share what they are hearing from God. Often it will be rather clear. The leader of this meeting then needs to verbally synthesize what has been named about each individual. If there is consensus, the group would go on to the next person. If not, some discussion or further prayer may be needed. The discernment meeting would end with a time of prayer.

Several steps may follow. For example, whoever conducted the conference could go back and talk further with the individual. The initiation minister would have to express honestly and delicately to the inquirer any reservations of the team, and see where this goes. This meeting must be approached with some openness to how the other will respond. Naming these reservations may evoke real movement of the Spirit within the inquirer, to which the discerning team needs to be open.

## Informal Discernment Processes

The discernment process that has just been described is just one possibility, and may occur in various ways. Many parishes do discernment more informally. Precatechumenate ministers express concerns about an inquirer as the concern arises. Or perhaps the initiation coordinator becomes aware that a problem exists. The coordinator or another initiation minister talks with the inquirer about the concern and sees where this leads. Another possibility may simply be that whoever has the one-on-one conversations with the inquirers talks to the precatechumenate leaders individually to hear their perception of the movement of God in the person. Then the individual conferences occur. There is simply an invitation for the inquirer to notice what is happening within from the experience of the precatechumenate, and to name the desire to more formally explore full membership in the Church. It is necessary that we approach this moment of potential readiness for the catechumenate with a discerning prayerful attitude open to how God might move during the time of discernment. We must also be able to talk with other initiation ministers and inquirers in truth and in trust.

Keep in mind the earlier image of discernment as a time of listening to the truth that is within and experienced, of honestly naming what is heard and seen, and of holding all of this openly before God to sense God's invitation and direction. This is what we are doing during this time of discernment in precatechumenate. For the most part, it will seem clear who has the needed signs of readiness for the catechumenate, who has some of them though not as fully developed as they might be, and who does not have these signs. In sensing the presence or absence of these qualities, the life story and culture of the inquirer are taken into account. Where are these signs as evident as possible given who this person is, and where is more needed? Usually, if there is readiness for the catechumenate, a sense exists that the inquirer's heart is opening. By this time, the inquirer has grown in a trusting relationship with the precatechumenate leaders enough to begin letting some of the real self be known. And a true desire for a deeper relationship with God and Church is alive and visible.

Discernment is easy if all those who wish to move into the catechumenate are indeed ready. It becomes difficult when they are not, particularly if they are intent on becoming a catechumen at this time. Often, we have a sense that more time is needed in the precatechumenate from the lack of participation in sessions, from the manner of engagement at given sessions and/or from things we are hearing the inquirer say or not say. The hope is that reservations about the inquirer moving on to the catechumenate can be expressed in a supportive way rather than that there is something wrong or lacking in the person.

Often a combination of a concrete behavior or experience of the person coupled with an "I" statement is helpful. For example: "Sue, I know you really want this faith journey. But I'm questioning whether this is the right time for you to move on to the catechumenate given the family concerns you've been sharing." This freed her to say, "You're right. I want it, but in a way I'd be cheating myself out of all that this experience can be for me if I move into the catechumenate now."

From the time of the initial conference when someone contacts the parish, it is important to convey that this is an individualized faith journey with various rituals that will be celebrated when there is an appropriate readiness. We want to communicate from this first conference that though, there may be hopes of being initiated the next Easter Vigil, more time might be needed. We invite people to come into the process being open to God's timing, and want to listen with individuals for this timing. If this understanding has been voiced from the beginning, it is much easier to talk with them about concerns or reservations as the process unfolds.

## Language Conveys Process

At times, the language used in precatechumenate sessions and in individual conferences belies this sense of individual timing and discernment. For example, initiation ministers sometimes talk about "this group" and "last year's group." These words imply that all individuals move along in the process together. Phrases such as "when you receive the sacraments at Easter" set up a specific time expectation. If we truly want the timing of this process to be individual and open to discernment, then we must pay attention to what we communicate by the language we use.

## Acting on Team Instincts

As initiation ministers, we pay attention to what people are saying and what is occurring in their lives. It is helpful for us to check in periodically with one another to discuss what is happening for persons in the precatechumenate. Usually, if we have questions it takes us awhile to name them. We may have a gut instinct but not at first know what we are feeling. If we talk with other initiation ministers about what we are sensing in the various persons, it helps us name our experience, clarify what we are picking up, and where we may even be off a bit. The person (or persons) conducting the conferences should keep in contact with the inquirer. As soon as real concerns arise, the initiation minister needs to set up a conference to talk about them—the earlier the better. We can get into trouble by putting off this step. There is little time to invite the inquirer to look at the reality of his or her journey if the concerns are expressed shortly before the Rite of Acceptance is being celebrated, and everyone else is ready to move on to the catechumenate.

## Continual Discernment

Though definite moments of discernment can be named in the precatechumenate, initiation ministers begin to see that the whole time is one of discernment. From the initial phone call onward, the person who is inquiring and the initiation ministers—both in precatechumenate sessions and conferences, as well as in living throughout the week—are listening and sifting through where this movement of God is happening and leading. The more comfortable the initiation ministers are with discerning and naming the various realities within their own lives, the more at ease they will be in talking with inquirers about their lives. This holds true even when this conversation may be delicate. We initiation ministers who are discerning about God's action in the person need to be truthful, free to listen to each other, and in touch with this discernment process in our own lives. Above all, we need to trust where God leads in this process.

### For Reflection

In what ways do inquirers pick up from your coordinator and initiation ministers a sense of discerning God's movement and timing in this faith journey?

How do you presently discern the readiness of inquirers to celebrate the Rite of Acceptance into the Order of Catechumens?

From your experience with specific individuals, name the qualities you sense in a person who is ready to move into the catechumenate.

What are the next steps for your initiation ministers to better incorporate an attitude of discernment into the precatechumenate?

# Chapter 5

# Discernment in the Catechumenate Period

Discernment in the catechumenate pervades the entire period from the celebration of the Rite of Acceptance into the Order of Catechumens until the Rite of Election. For the already-baptized and uncatechized persons who have a similar formation to that of catechumens, this period embraces the celebration of the Rite of Welcoming to the celebration of the Call to Continuing Conversion (401, 402). A fixed time ends the period of the catechumenate—the Rite of Election—which is on or near the First Sunday of Lent. The length of the catechumenate still varies depending on when and how often the Rite of Acceptance is celebrated, and which year the person participates in the Rite of Election.

We must remember that the *Rite of Christian Initiation of Adults* envisions a year-round catechumenate. Every Sunday of the year, catechumens are participating with the assembly in the Liturgy of the Word and being dismissed. Catechumens come into the catechumenate at various times when the Rite of Acceptance is celebrated. On the first Sunday of Lent *some* of the catechumens are declared elect to be initiated at the next Easter Vigil. Others continue in the catechumenate. The period of the catechumenate is to extend for at least one year (*National Statutes*, 6). The length of the catechumenate cannot be set beforehand (NS, 76). Ongoing discernment is needed to know whether the Rite of Election should be celebrated for an unbaptized person this year, or whether it is appropriate to wait.

## Seeds Are Planted

These are some of the more technical aspects of the RCIA. Keep in mind the heart and value underneath them. We are being encouraged to allow time for the real faith journey of the person to occur. During the precatechumenate, the inquirer gets in touch with his or her faith and inner life more closely and names and articulates what is there. As the inquirer experiences the initial conversion, it is like the ground is being tilled, broken up, or softened. This initial conversion is in place as the person celebrates the Rite of Acceptance into the Order of Catechumens. The longer period of the catechumenate is like the growing season. The soil is aerated and fertilized. Plants already growing are cared for and pruned. New seeds are planted, watered, nurtured. As plants spring up and grow larger, they are given the needed care. It takes time for the plants to grow strong. Some plants require a longer growing period than others. Gradually they grow toward the sun.

Discernment in the period of the catechumenate involves an ongoing naming of and paying attention to the growth that is happening. The concern of discernment in this period is not only the determination of who goes on to celebrate the Rite of Election this Lent. It is much larger. Discernment is learned as a way of life in the week-by-week experience of the catechumenate. Coordinator, sponsor, and catechists assist the catechumen to live as a discerning disciple, naming the movements of God's Spirit throughout this time.

## The Rite of Acceptance into the Order of Catechumens

The first moment of discernment in this catechumenate period occurs with the dismissal at the Rite of Acceptance. With its powerful symbols, this celebration touches into a new level of the earth. Here, the catechumens often have a very deep experience of God, of Christ, of Church, of cross, and of the meaning of discipleship. When the new catechumens gather with the catechist after the dismissal, the catechist helps them name what they experienced in the rite. The catechist assists them through some of the listening skills described earlier to notice and articulate the movements of God's Spirit that they experienced in the Rite of Acceptance. Something new and deeper happens as these movements are articulated and shared. Catechists need not be timid or hesitant as emotion and depth of experience come forth. This experience, articulation, and sharing prepare the soil even more for the action of God during the catechumenate.

## Aim of the Catechumenate

The first few lines of description of the catechumenate state that the aim of this period is "training . . . in the Christian life" (75). These words set the broader context for discernment during this period. For to be trained in the life of Christians means ongoing practice in living as disciples and in listening to where God calls, to the movements within of God's Spirit. The rite names movements of God's Spirit that we might anticipate hearing about from the catechumens. We need to listen for catechumens' descriptions of how they "turn more readily to God in prayer," "bear witness to the faith," "keep their hopes set on Christ," "follow supernatural inspiration in their deeds," and "practice love of neighbor, even at the cost of self-renunciation" (75.2). We wait to hear stories of how catechumens "spread the Gospel and build up the Church by the witness of their lives" (75.4).

Many real-life descriptions of these phrases come forth in the weekly catechumenal sessions: "I feel as if I pray all the time now. God is there with me—in me—and I talk to God all through the day." "People at work can't believe I'm becoming Catholic. Some of them make critical remarks. It doesn't bother me, though. I know what I'm doing is right for me. There are a lot of misconceptions about the Catholic Church. I tell them what I'm finding." In times of pain or sorrow, we hear catechumens say, "In the past I would have been devastated. I think I would have fallen apart. But now that I have my relationship with Christ, I know I'll get through this." "People around me tell me I shouldn't change jobs. I know it's a risk. But I've prayed, and inside I know this is right and God will be with me. I really believe it will go well for me." "I'm even nice to those I don't particularly like. I used to avoid some of my neighbors, but now I can see how they're hurting. I want to be more compassionate to them to lighten their burden a little. Maybe I can make a difference in their lives." "I've been handing out sandwiches to the homeless every Thursday with my sponsor. I'm sensing as I talk with these people that I am really no different than they are. These are truly my sisters and brothers." These are some examples. As you read the words of the rite and these words above, perhaps ways you have heard catechumens naming these movements in their lives will come to you. The deepening of these movements continues throughout the catechumenate.

## Forming Discerning Disciples

Discernment during this ongoing time of the catechumenate has a pervasive and somewhat informal quality. With the focus given to "training . . . in the Christian life" (75) it becomes implicitly necessary to teach catechumens how to discern, how to listen for the movement of God's Spirit within all arenas of life. Discernment is taught by doing. When we say we are discerning it is important that this is what we are doing and not simply making a decision.

A catechumen learns to live as a discerning disciple in some of the following ways. He or she may dialogue with a catechist about a discernment question in an area of his or her life. The catechist may explore with the catechumen, particularly with reference to Scripture and tradition, where the movement toward God and life may be. Perhaps the catechist would name aspects of the question to be brought to prayer. Through sharing and ongoing relationship, a sponsor may be privy to various questions with which the catechumen is wrestling. A sponsor can facilitate a deeper personal exploration of feelings, "voices," "shoulds," and desires within the catechumen. A catechumen may talk with other initiation ministers in ordinary conversation about a discernment he or she is making. We need to be ready to notice when this happens to give attention to what is brought up rather than simply commenting. Catechumens will learn how to discern as they see and hear we initiation ministers speak of our experiences of discerning God's movement and invitation. Even without the language of discernment, catechumens will understand the sifting through of what leads one closer to God through sharings of sponsors, catechists, and other initiation ministers. An initiation minister who has the gift of being a discerning listener may offer the opportunity for periodic conferences throughout the time of the catechumenate.

## Before Celebrating Election

The RCIA explains what the Church expects as the time of the catechumenate comes to a close. Before the Rite of Election is celebrated, the catechumens are to "have undergone a conversion in mind and in action and to have developed a sufficient acquaintance with Christian teaching as well as a spirit of faith and charity" (120). They are also to have the intention of receiving the sacraments of the Church (120). Again, rather than using the language of discernment, the rite speaks of a "judgment about the catechumens' state of formation and progress" that is to involve "the bishop, priests, deacons, catechists, godparents, and the entire community" (121). The following paragraph further specifies that there is to be a "deliberation . . . by priests, deacons, and catechists . . . godparents and representatives of the local community" (122). And, as is essential to any real discernment, the statement is made that "catechumens may also take part" in the deliberations (122).

The Rite of Election, a pivotal moment, is not meant to be a mere formality. It therefore requires a real judgment or deliberation about the progress of each of the catechumens. The discernment needed encompasses four areas: whether there has been a real conversion in mind and in action, whether there is a sufficient acquaintance with Christian teaching, whether the catechumens have taken on a spirit of faith and charity, and whether they have the intention of receiving the sacraments of the Church. The discernment process is meant to include members of the local community who are not involved in a specific ministry of the initiation process as well as sponsors and other initiation ministers. The following paragraphs will attend to these aspects of discernment needed before the celebration of election.

## Importance of Election

The Rite of Election is "founded on the election by God, in whose name the Church acts" (119). Discernment at this moment of the journey is about the Church naming the concrete evidence that God is truly electing the person. Is there evidence or not? As one is named and declared elected by God, all is different for the person. This action and movement of God in the person has already been happening. Yet a new reality occurs in the naming, ritualizing, and celebration within the community. Care and concern are invited that the underlying truth of what is being ritualized exists. The godparents/sponsors are called upon to give testimony to this truth. They name their sense of the election of God in this person through specific experiences and awarenesses of God's gifts being lived out in the person's life.

## Conversion of Mind and Action

This election of God happening in the person is the object of the discernment before the celebration of the Rite of Election. The conversion of mind and action looked for implies a real turning to God's ways and values in specific choices. The person is not just using spiritual language, but is making and living concrete choices. Often, after a period of time in the catechumenate, people begin grappling with some of their deeper life issues and pain. They deal with broken relationships, especially those in family and marriages. They find real shifts in how they operate in business. They work with the effects of their family-of-origin issues. They move into greater inner freedom and living in truth. As these changes happen, they find more desire and energy to be of service in the broader community. They become more attentive to and active in justice concerns within their neighborhoods, city, and world. And beneath all of this movement is a deeper and deeper life of relationship with God. The "spirit of faith and charity" pervades all areas of the catechumen's life.

## Acquaintance with Christian Teaching

The concern for whether the catechumen has a "sufficient acquaintance with Christian teaching" can be looked at in different ways. The catechists or other initiation ministers will have a sense of whether the essential aspects of Christian faith have been talked about in the catechumenal sessions. The coordinator will be aware of how long the person has been a catechumen and what parts of the Gospel formed the basis for the particular catechumenate experience. The sponsors and catechists will also have a sense of the catechumen's acquaintance with Christian teaching by how he or she talks about the Gospel affecting daily life. In addition, the catechumen needs to let the coordinator know whether he or she has received what is needed, or feels some lack. Hopefully, the catechumens will leave the catechumenate still hungering for more awareness of the Gospel.

## Intention of Receiving the Sacraments

Most catechumens are in the process of initiation because they
want to receive the sacraments, yet this area should not be taken
for granted. I recall one woman who, several weeks before the
Rite of Election, expressed a concern that, though wanting
to believe, she currently was unable to accept that in receiving
Eucharist she would be really receiving Jesus. As we spoke,
she realized that this belief would be a gift for which she would
ask God. As she opened herself to this gift, God responded.
Accompanying this growing conversion in the person is usually
a deepening desire for oneness with Christ in the sacraments.
As we attempt to discern the movement of God within the person, we do not want to overlook the catechumen's articulation of
a desire for the sacraments.

## Involvement of the Local Community

Interestingly, the RCIA invites representatives from the local
community, from the broader Church, along with those with
particular initiation ministries, to be part of the determination-
of-readiness process for the celebration of the Rite of Election.
The first liturgical rite, that of Acceptance into the Order of
Catechumens, literally brings the catechumens into the Church,
the community of believers. This Church pledges to walk with
and assist these catechumens on their journey to Christ. The
catechumens interact with persons from the broader community
in their daily life. Evidence of the conversion that is happening
will be lived in experiences outside of the catechumenal sessions
as well as within. The apostolic witness and life of service to which
the catechumens are invited will be noticed and shared with many
in the community. The Rite of Election enables the entire assembly as well as the godparents to affirm the signs of election in the
catechumens. So, it is not surprising and indeed appropriate for
members of the local community to be part of the discernment
of election.

The discernment needed before the Rite of Election, then, will include various members of the community. Sponsors who have walked closely with the catechumens will be a good resource for naming how they have heard and seen the signs of God's election happening. Catechists and various initiation ministers will have experiences to bring to the discernment. Several weeks before the celebration of the Rite of Election, the discerning listener may have a conference to help the catechumen name where the movement has happened and where he or she may still be holding out on God. And, as the RCIA suggests, members of the community who know one or more of the catechumens may be invited to state what they experience in the person. The goal of the discernment with sponsors, initiation ministers, local community, discerning listener, and catechumen will be to name concrete ways the "conversion of mind and action" has taken place (120). Some of the elements named in paragraphs 75.2 and 75.4 specify further the forms this conversion takes.

## Discernment Processes

Various processes could be used and may even change from year to year given the numbers of catechumens, catechists, and other needs. For example, initiation ministers who will be responsible for the discernment may each take a few catechumens they will represent. Each could then contact local community members whose names were given by catechumen, the sponsor, and catechists and invite them to name how they experience these traits of the Christian life happening within the catechumen. The discerning listeners may have an individual conference with the catechumen to help articulate the deeper life that has been unfolding. The initiation ministers responsible for the discernment will then come together in a context of prayerful listening and present what they are hearing. These members then would need to name and articulate what surfaces in their listening in prayer. They would continue to talk and pray until some agreement is reached. If there are concerns or questions, the discerning listener would need to bring this back to the catechumen, again with a spirit of openness and listening. The affirmation also needs to be taken back to the catechumen.

Another scenario may involve bringing all sponsors, catechists, and initiation ministers together. Since this would be a larger group, it seems preferable to glean any input from the broader community and bring it to this gathering. In a context of prayer the sponsors could be led through a reflection on the person companioned in relationship to the aspects of the Christian life named in paragraph 75. The sponsors would then be invited to name how they see the evidence of the conversion in mind and action. Catechists and other initiation ministers would divide up into groups and reflect on the catechumens they know best. The discerning listener would also bring what has been learned in conferences with the various catechumens. However, confidentiality is required unless permission has been granted by the catechumen to share information in the discernment process. After a period of prayerful listening there would be a naming of affirmations or concerns. When clarity is reached, the input needs to be brought back to the catechumen in prayerful dialogue.

When questions arise about the progress a catechumen is making, they need to be brought to the person as early as possible. Obviously, this should be done with care and honesty. It is helpful to name concrete behaviors that cannot be misinterpreted as a judgment: "We've been noticing that you're coming late in recent weeks. Could you help us understand why? We're concerned that there may be some conflict in your family about you being in this process." "Most of the time during our sessions you seem to not participate. I've been wondering if they are not meaningful for you or if you have some concern. What would you say is happening for you in the catechumenate?"

Depending on how the conversation moves, it may be appropriate to suggest a longer period of catechumenate: "I hear that with all you are doing right now that this feels like a burden, another thing to do. Maybe you need to slow this process down and take some time so that when you do move on to the Rite of Election and the Easter sacraments it will be true to what's happening in your life. What would that be like for you?" This type of honest conversation builds on trust levels that began early in the process. It also presupposes the sense of process and discernment being brought up and lived from the beginning of the precatechumenate.

## Sponsors: A Great Resource

Sponsors are a valuable resource in this discernment process. They usually have a close relationship with the catechumen as they journey together week by week. Sponsor formation, therefore, needs to include listening skills to enable him or her to facilitate the catechumen's deeper articulation of life and God experience.

Sponsors know what is happening in the person's life and faith journey. They may share their reflection on the catechumen they are companioning in relationship to named characteristics of the Christian life with a team member, or be present at an actual time of discernment. The input could be written or oral. Involving sponsors in this process also helps prepare them for their role of giving witness at the Rite of Election and/or Sending for Election, and calls forth a new depth of their role as church.

## Reverence and Carefulness

No matter what process is involved, we must keep before us the sense that each person is sacred and God's movement in the individual is to be reverenced. God's call or election will be evidenced uniquely in each person. Some will be very articulate and greatly moved to actions of justice. Others will be quieter and the changes in their lives will be subtle. Great care must be taken that we reverence each person, that some deep confidences are respected, that information that may hurt another is not given out imprudently, and that only those who can truly enter into this type of discernment are invited to do so. Those who are not experienced in dealing with matters of the heart may not be the best discerners. A discernment process is needed that will be respectful of the individual catechumens and will function well in the particular local community.

## For Reflection

What is your present practice of discernment during the period of the catechumenate? In what ways do you envision discernment as an integral part of this entire period?

How do your catechumens learn to be discerning disciples? What is one further step your initiation ministers might take for this to happen more fully in your parish?

What are you coming to understand more fully about discernment before the celebration of the Rite of Election?

# Chapter 6

# Discernment during Purification and Enlightenment

In the Rite of Election the bishop declares a catechumen to be a member of the elect who will be initiated at the next Easter Vigil. The bishop acts in the name of the Church, which acts in the name of God. Once one is named as an elect of God, this state remains. The discernment of who participates in the Easter sacraments is complete.

## Discernment Is at the Heart of this Period

Discernment in the life of the elect, though, has only begun. For the elect now embark on the period of purification and enlightenment, only to lead to the sacraments of initiation and the full living of the Christian life. Discernment within the elect intensifies during this period, which has as its focus a purification of their minds and hearts from all that still holds them back from Christ. This time is also intended to more fully enlighten them with a more intimate and deeper knowledge of Christ. And so discernment or sifting through the spirits operative deep within the elect is at the very heart of this period.

## Discerning Roots of Sin and of Graciousness

The discernment required at this moment of the journey goes deeper into the fiber of the being of the elect. This is a time of opening even further to God and God's ways, of letting go of patterns of sin and attachments and old attitudes that keep the elect from living more fully with and in Christ. This is a time of noticing and choosing to move away from ways the elect have participated in social and cultural evil, of falling more radically into the being of Christ.

Looking at the rite that is celebrated at the conclusion of each period gives a vision of what is to happen. This period of purification and enlightenment has its fulfillment in the Easter sacraments. Just prior to the celebration of Baptism, the elect clearly choose to live through, with, and in Christ in stating the baptismal promises. The elect reject the way of sin and promise to live as children of God, as children of light. In the early Church, these baptismal promises were an even clearer pronouncement of the choice of Christ over evil. The elect literally turned toward the west, the place where darkness comes, and renounced the power of evil in their lives. Then they turned toward the east, the place of the rising sun, and claimed their fidelity to Christ.[1]

This turning away from sin and in the direction of Christ is what is to occur more radically during purification and enlightenment. The impetus for this turning is set clearly in the Scriptures on the First Sunday of Lent, the time when the Rite of Election and/or Sending for Election is celebrated. This meaning of a willingness to move more fully toward the Easter sacraments, and thus to literally turn one's entire life over to God, is intimately connected with discerning the hold sin has so as to be able to choose to live with God in Christ.

## Jesus Discerned Sin and Grace

In each of the three years of readings, the Gospel for this First Sunday of Lent is of Jesus being tempted in the desert. In year A, we have the poignancy of Adam and Eve choosing sin over God's ways and Jesus choosing God's ways when tempted in the desert. The Gospel words suggest Jesus discerns and chooses faithfulness to God. Jesus is led by the Spirit into the desert, a spirit-filled place, a place of sifting through spirits, of discernment. Jesus remained there, figuratively, for forty days and nights. The account of Jesus' encounter with the evil one makes it sound easy. The evil one said one thing, and Jesus responded with faithfulness to God. Jesus was very likely using the time in the desert to sift through all the different spirits. How was his mission to be fulfilled? Were there any shortcuts or easy ways? What would happen to him in the process? How faithful would God be in the face of what could lie ahead? In hindsight, naming the choices made does not readily manifest the struggle and discernment involved.

## The Elect Discern Sin and Grace

The elect have this forty-day period of purification and enlighten-ment to discern spirits. They, too, are led by the Spirit into the desert to look more deeply into their inner selves, a process that uncovers places of woundedness and sinfulness, as well as of wholeness and holiness. Seeing their wounds and sinfulness is not intended to provoke blame and undue guilt. Rather, it is done in the light of being named elect of God. The elect know the experi-ence of being personally loved by God. In this light of God's love they can now open themselves to see who they are before God. This revelation includes seeing themselves as holy, as children of God created in God's image and likeness, and seeing all that keeps them from greater wholeness and closer relationship with God. The analogy is similar to what happens when we turn on the light in a darkened room, especially if the room is unfamil-iar. Before the light is turned on, all the furniture and objects are there. But when it is turned on, all that is in the room can then be seen. What is good and valuable to keep or restore, and what needs to be discarded is now visible. Looking at the results of the hurts and wounds of life, and at ways of participating in evil is not done to name what's wrong with the elect. Rather, it's the sense of being in deep relationship with God. God, who loves, gently shows or illuminates all that keeps them from living fully as children of light. And an inner desire emerges to let God lovingly heal the wounds and bring about fuller life.

The elect begin to identify thought, emotional, and behavioral patterns that have long been ingrained in them. Perhaps they always judge others' motives or unconsciously tell themselves they are never good enough. Perhaps they have allowed fear to keep them from letting their true voice be spoken. Perhaps they have always pretended everything's okay without letting themselves acknowledge their painful, though real, feelings. Perhaps they are success driven or neglectful of their own needs and desires. They may discover within themselves a prejudice based on race, economics, sexuality, or gender. They see how their values have been shaped by the media or materialism. They recognize how they participate in or are caught in unjust systems. They sense a new connection with all of creation and ways they have not cared for the earth. They name how they have been affected by their family of origin. The elect begin to see in a new way their connection with all of God's people, with women and men who truly are their sisters and brothers throughout their city and the entire globe.

The elect begin to let themselves name the one or two areas within that they have been afraid of or unwilling to look at until now. Words such as *Ask me anything but that* express this part of self that has been held back from God. At times, there is a deep hurt that has been experienced and retained. Perhaps they have not forgiven or accepted a part of themselves, or a way they lived earlier in their lives that they are ashamed of and wish had never happened. The invitation for freedom and wholeness involves letting God's light and love shine even on this part of their lives. The elect find that God loves them not only when they are "good" or whole, but even in their sinfulness or woundedness. God loves them through and through.

## Struggle in Opening Further to God

Letting God reveal or illumine what is within is not easy and usually does not occur without struggle. The elect take a step
at a time of opening their hands and hearts more fully to God, and
feel God's love and trust in all that they have been experiencing.
They gradually risk vulnerability in one more area, then another.
Then there may be some holding back, a desire to withdraw to safety.
Then another moment of trust and risk occurs. As the elect continue to let God's love into all the parts of themselves, a healing
occurs of past hurts that had been closed off. The elect become more
and more bonded to this God who liberates and heals and knows
and loves them. They are at once drawn into living God's love more
deeply in many real ways in their lives.

## Scrutinies Integral to Discernment of This Period

The scrutinies are a gift to aid in this discernment process. The
words in the *Rite of Christian Initiation of Adults* present the sense
of discernment clearly:

> The scrutinies are meant to uncover, then heal all that is weak,
> defective, or sinful in the hearts of the elect; to bring out, then
> strengthen all that is upright, strong, and good. For the scrutinies
> are celebrated in order to deliver the elect from the power of sin
> and Satan, to protect them against temptation, and to give them
> strength in Christ, who is the way, the truth, and the life. (141)

The Gospels of the Third, Fourth, and Fifth Sundays of
Lent in Year A of the Lectionary are foundational to the scrutinies,
and provide images that facilitate the discernment of spirits
operating within the elect. In the Gospel of the Samaritan
woman at the well on the Third Sunday of Lent (John 4:4–42),
in being known and accepted as she is, the woman is freed. She
enthusiastically invites the townspeople to see the one who
told her everything she ever did, the one who knows her deeply
and accepts her as she is. The experience this woman had with

Christ, who took the time and occasion to relate to her, was that she was known in her truth, loved as she is, and in turn freed.

In the Gospel of the man born blind (John 9:1–41), we are tuned into understandings of spiritual blindness. We hear of a man who not only gained physical sight, but was given true sight in Christ. The Gospel of the raising of Lazarus (John 11:1–44) brings us in touch with life and death as Lazarus is called forth from his tomb. The words of Jesus to Lazarus, "come out!" (John 11:43) and to the gathered community to untie him so he may go free, resound with poignancy. These powerful symbols of coming out of one's tomb to new life, and being untied by one another leading to freedom, make room for felt connections and understandings of personal inner life and life in community.

These same Gospels help the elect encounter Christ and be illumined with who Christ is. Christ liberates and frees us, and is truly living water. Christ indeed makes the sightless see, and the seeing blind. Christ is truly the light of the world. Christ brings back to life, and is intent on unbinding and freeing. Christ is the resurrection and the life.

The scrutinizing is not done by the Church, or even by the elect. God is the One who scrutinizes hearts and lives. Through these Gospels and the entire celebration of the scrutinies, the elect experience God scrutinizing their hearts.

## Purification and Enlightenment Occur Together

As the hearts of the elect are laid bare before God, God is able to heal the places of sin and woundedness. The elect become more fully joined to Christ. The opening, healing, and being illumined with Christ are not separate moments, but happen simultaneously. The elect begin to want no other water than the living water who is Christ, and can no longer look through blind eyes when they have seen. Seeing only becomes possible in connection with the real light who is Christ. And it is no longer satisfying to stay entombed or be part of the binding of others. The elect desire to live in greater integrity and inner freedom. Christ is true life and the elect become more and more united with Christ.

## The Scrutiny Dismissal Session

The catechist who leads the elect forth from the scrutiny and encourages them to name what is taking place inside is key in this time of discernment. Tears and stories frequently pour out: "A few weeks ago I finally said I was sorry to a woman I was forced to terminate from her job a few years ago. I know how hard that loss was for her and how it affected her life. She said she forgives me. But now, today, I believe I forgave myself. I just have to open my heart and hand it over to God. And that's God's grace, not me." "Today was hard. It's deep. It's a whole new level of searching that I'm doing. It's difficult, but it's so good. Thank you." "I've heard you ask over and over, 'How am I experiencing God?' Now I know what that means. I hear and feel God inside in a new way." "I see how I've held on to my sin, to my guilt for my sin. I'm understanding that we all walk together. The guilt of my sin is not as heavy. I can let go of it. And, I'm not alone." "At first the letting go of control was hard. But the more I do it, the easier it is. Now I want to just keep turning everything over to God." "I'm different. I am now able to name sin such as racism and sexism of which I'm ashamed. I really want God to change me. Even as I say this, I know my heart is different." A catechist with some skill in being a discerning listener will astutely give simple reflective statements, stay with the emotion, allow silence, and invite further attention to and naming of these deep movements of God. The celebration of a scrutiny is a powerful ritual that unleashes deep grace in the elect. Leaders of the reflection need to be comfortable with and deeply attuned to these movements of the heart. The naming of and further praying with these movements allow God's grace to unfold more deeply within the elect.

## Discernment Occurs in Many Ways

Discernment, which happens in the depth of the heart, and choosing faithfulness permeates this time rather than occurring in a specific moment or way. The medium for the discernment is the celebration of the scrutinies with intercessions naming the sin being turned over to God and proclaiming Christ as living water, giver of sight, and full life, the laying on of hands, and prayer. The medium is also the Gospel and homily and entire Liturgy of the Word. The medium is the ongoing prayer and sharing with godparent and others that arises out of the liturgy. The medium is the naming and proclamation of the deep movements and shifts within attributed to God's grace alone. The medium is the sharing of these graced experiences with other believers in the community of the Church. Though not required, offering a conference with a discerning listener to process more deeply what is happening inside the elect is a further way to attend to this discernment.

Discernment during this period helps to ready the elect to more fully experience their Baptism into the death and Resurrection of Christ. Sin and sinfulness lose their power and control as the elect truly turn themselves over to Christ. As they move toward the time of celebration of the Easter sacraments, all that the elect desire is to live more fully through, with, and in Christ.

### For Reflection

From your own participation in the liturgy on the Sundays of Lent, and in particular being present at the celebration of scrutinies, what is your experience of discernment of spirits that occurs within yourself?

Name some stories you have heard from the elect during this period that tell you of the discernment of spirits that is happening within them.

How may a catechist or leader of sessions with the elect facilitate a deepening of the discernment that occurs during this period?

# Chapter 7

# Mystagogia and Beyond

The experience of the Easter sacraments is deep and profoundly changes the neophytes. They literally see and live life differently. They are caught up in life with God in Christ and live their days noticing "Spirit happenings." The energy, excitement, possibility, and new moment we read about in the Acts of the Apostles that describe the Spirit alive in the early Church are happening once again. It's as if the neophytes are walking around with a new set of glasses whereby they are utterly attuned to this same Spirit alive and active in our midst.

## Evidence of an Alive Spirit

Neophytes share experiences and cannot wait to tell stories during the mystagogia period. When asked about her Baptism, Beth, a woman in her early twenties, says, "I was just me. In the water it was like the heavens and everything opened up to me. Now, I'm part of everything—God, creation, and everyone." This description reveals something about what the transformation that occurs in Baptism really is. It's a shift in one's being at a deep level and is manifest in surprising ways. Jim, who works in maintenance, excitedly says, "I have to tell you what happened this week. Coming home from work when I'm hot, dirty, and tired, I found a purse on the street. I went to the house. No one was home. I went to the police station. They were astounded that someone brought in a purse. I said, 'It's the Christian thing to do.' I don't know where those words came from. I've never thought them. It's amazing!" When hearing such stories and experiences,

the catechist, godparent, and initiation ministers are able to facilitate a deeper meaning by using skills of discerning listening. If
initiation ministers pay attention when these kinds of experiences
are shared, the meaning and feelings will continue to come forth.
Without inviting and listening deeply, these movements of the
Spirit may be missed or not fully appropriated. The discernment
called for at this moment is simply listening, highlighting, and
appreciating this powerful Spirit occurrence.

## Discerning Mission

The understanding that mission occurs at Baptism is well-known.
The experience is real and many neophytes want to relate it over
and over. They want to tell the community, and the parish all
that has happened in them. They want to express and share their
joy and gratitude. Concomitantly, a new moment in the journey
begins to unfold. One neophyte, Sharon, said just two weeks after
her Baptism: "I was looking forward to my baptism as a time of
fulfillment, when I would have all that I need and want. Only a
few days later I realized 'I can't rest here. I must go out. I must
do something.'" The movement outward happens. A new time
of discernment begins. In what direction is God calling the
neophyte? Often, the immediate response is to get the neophytes
involved in liturgical or other parish ministries. There is a tendency to act on the excitement too quickly, before any real inner
discernment occurs.

## Areas of Concern in Discerning Mission

Several areas of concern may appear at this time. One is that
if the energy is moved toward resolution too fast, the full impact
of what is happening within may be missed. The moment must
be relished and deeply absorbed to provide the depth needed for
the future. Neophytes need encouragement to become more fully
aware of the postbaptismal experience. What are the effects of this
deep joy and gratitude they feel? What changes inside them and

in their life do they notice? How do they see the Spirit moving in their family and work environment? What's it like to live being this aware of the Spirit's actions?

Another potential area of concern is that by immediately moving into a ministry within the parish, the neophyte may miss the Spirit's call to mission beyond the parish walls to the neighborhood or people in the inner city. Hopefully, some of this missionary activity has already begun in the catechumenate period. If not, parish staff and initiation ministers need to be careful not to exert pressure just to fill slots in the parish, to satisfy staff concerns. Naming the needs of the parish or opportunities available is part of the information needed in discernment. Yet, there is a difference between the neophyte saying, "I can do this" and knowing inside "this is where the Spirit is inviting me." Neophytes may be called to spend more time in prayer or give more of their energy to their families. They may be thrust into sharing their faith and experience in informal ways within and outside the parish. Neophytes may feel called to serve the poor more wholeheartedly or to work for the just rights of others. Initiation ministers who discern with neophytes need to keep a broad vision of mission and ministry.

A third area of concern involving moving too quickly is that this is simply a time of discernment, of sifting through the spirits to see where God is really calling and inviting. Some individual attention with a discerning listener is much more advantageous and desirable at this moment of the journey than presenting parish ministries to all of the neophytes together. Godparents or initiation ministers may talk with neophytes to help them become aware of specific resources and opportunities for ministry. This needs to be done with a spirit of exploration and freedom, avoiding any pressure or bias. There is a tendency to jump into a doing mentality rather than an acting in response to inner promptings of the Spirit. There does not need to be a long period of time before movement to mission occurs. Rather, it is the process that is important. The movement to mission comes from the specific way one is being impelled by the Spirit. What is the ministry to which the neophyte feels drawn? Is the neophyte able to name what it is that draws him or her to this ministry? Does the neophyte desire this ministry out of an inner prompting or because the neophyte believes for some reason he or she "should" do this? What gifts has the Spirit given? Is the neophyte willing to listen and wait for God to give the leadings for ministry? Whoever discerns with the neophyte helps him or her name the inner experience and listens with him or her for God's movement in freedom.

## Living as a Discerning Disciple

If we believe that discernment is an essential aspect of discipleship, then we must be consistent at this postbaptismal time. Helping the neophyte discern a direction for the mission opening up in Baptism will deepen the inner understanding of the process of listening to the Spirit. Discernment at this moment will reinforce—or take away from—what previously has been perceived by the neophyte about living as a discerning disciple.

## Ongoing Discernment

As the mystagogical time begins to extend past Pentecost, new moments of discernment will arise. The intense experience of the Spirit eases. What does the neophyte need to stay deeply attuned to life with God? (Old ways of living that are no longer life-giving or even former sinful behavior may creep back at this time.) Living into the baptismal faith of life with Christ will need discernment as various situations and life events present themselves. Without the weekly sessions, the neophyte will need to take more individual responsibility for hearing the invitation in the Word and living Eucharist. What's it like to be just another member of the Church? How is ministry unfolding? Where is the Spirit leading now? Some of these areas will come up in the first year of ongoing mystagogia. Catechists who lead these sessions

need to be attuned to the areas of discernment that present themselves to neophytes.

During this extended time of mystagogia, some neophytes
will seek more regular connection with the godparent/sponsor
or some one-on-one conversations with an initiation minister
to help them name and listen to their experience. During this
period, the role of the godparent/sponsor is much more informal
but no less important. The neophyte will be used to sharing and
processing inner experience with the godparent/sponsor, and
will usually look forward to opportunities for this to continue.
As the neophyte lives out this new life with Christ, the listening
presence is an ongoing support that the godparent/sponsor is
able to offer. As particular questions or new moments occur, and
as the more formal support of the initiation process comes to
an end, the godparent/sponsor continues to assist the neophyte
in discerning God's call.

As the neophyte continues to live into the daily unfolding
of the Christian life, the way of discernment will take on a new
enduring quality. Being a discerning disciple is the way of living
that will keep the neophyte deeply alive and attentive as life
with God in Christ matures.

## For Reflection

Name some "Spirit happenings" you have heard neophytes
share out of their baptismal experience and during the time
of mystagogia.

What is your sense of how to assist a neophyte in moving into
mission out of the inner promptings of the Spirit?

How do you invite the neophytes into a discernment that includes
a larger perspective of mission beyond the parish boundaries?

Chapter 8

# The Baptized Candidate

Many who present themselves with a desire to live as members of the Catholic Church have been baptized in another Christian tradition. In the early years of working with the initiation process, when ministers were learning the basics of the various rites and stages of the catechumenate, often no distinctions were made between the baptized and unbaptized. Over time, many trained and experienced coordinators, catechists, sponsors, liturgists, and presiders not only have gained necessary skills, but also have a deep appreciation of the initiation process. This understanding has led to the awareness that it is necessary to distinguish between those who are baptized and those who are not. A further distinction recognized is the extent to which the person is catechized. Anyone involved in initiation ministry knows that no two people in any of these categories are the same. Initiation ministers have begun to delve into Parts II.4 and II.5 of the RCIA for assistance and clarification about how a baptized candidate is brought into full communion with the Catholic Church.

## Validity of Baptism

Discernment with the baptized candidate involves some concrete issues. First, the initiation ministers must ascertain whether the person has been validly baptized. The initial interview is the place to get this information. For many, there is a simple yes or no. For others, it is more complex. A record or certificate of Baptism may not be available. The particular church of Baptism may not be in existence or may not have kept adequate records.

In some cases negative feelings toward Catholics makes getting needed data a delicate matter. Some Christian churches have a ritual of dedication or christening different from Baptism. The minister or recipient may not have intended Baptism. The Trinitarian formula or water may not have been used. The chancery office of the local diocese is a helpful resource for questions about particular circumstances.

## Level of Catechesis

When the person is already baptized, the next important question to answer is to what extent the person has been catechized. Each person is quite different in this area, ranging from almost no Christian formation to living fully as a Christian. Part II.4 addresses the situation of those who need a substantial amount of Christian formation. Part II.5 pertains to the circumstances of those who are actively living their Christian faith, and who may need formation in some specific aspects of Catholic tradition. We uphold their Baptism and in most circumstances do not re-baptize. In celebrating the rites, we are careful to choose appropriate words, prayer, and ritual in the formation process. The RCIA is clear that those already fully living their Christian faith are not to be asked to participate in an extensive program similar to the catechumenate (473, 477; *National Statutes,* 31).

Though there are many gray areas in determining what formation is appropriate, some tools are available to facilitate knowing how to proceed with the various individuals. Discernment is essential to know what is needed from person to person, and to recognize readiness for reception into full communion (478).

## Centrality of Conversion

Part I of the RCIA presents several essential dimensions of formation that facilitate conversion. Conversion is what determines readiness to progress from one stage of the initiation process to another. An initial conversion must be in place for the celebration of the Rite of Acceptance into the Order of Catechumens, and a conversion of mind and heart before one is declared elect for the Easter sacraments. In like manner, conversion will be what determines the timing of the baptized candidate's Rite of Welcome, Rite of the Call to Continuing Conversion, and/or Rite of Reception.

Paragraph 75 describes four areas of catechumenal formation. Catechesis accommodated to the liturgical year, living the Gospel message within the Christian community, participation in appropriate liturgical prayer, and apostolic service and witness give a basis for ascertaining what further formation is needed for conversion. Initiation ministers may wish to consider each of these areas, reflect on how they are addressed and experienced within the catechumenal process at your parish, and determine whether any of these are lacking in the candidate's experience and understanding.

The initiation minister conducting the initial interview, and follow-up conversations, asks about and listens for how these areas are part of the person's life. The focus of the conversations is not simply what the person knows intellectually. Rather, the goal is to find out how these components of faith are integrated into the person's life. For example, it is not enough that the candidate is familiar with the four Gospels. Rather, it is appropriate to engage in a deeper level of conversation about the ways he or she experiences living, dying, and rising with Christ in his or her own life. What particular teaching of Christ does he or she find compelling at this time, and what is his or her experience with this teaching?

In terms of catechetical content, most Christian denominations share the central elements of Christian faith found in the Nicene Creed. Degrees of variation exist in how the person understands the Trinity, and in his or her personal relationship with God. Beyond this, there is a degree of diversity depending on the candidate's particular Christian tradition. Some specific areas of Catholic tradition that need to be addressed may become obvious given the individual's particular Christian background. The understanding of Scripture may tend toward fundamentalism. Sacraments may or may not be part of the candidate's Christian faith. Some denominations see the role of Mary and the saints very differently. For many, the office of the pope and the teaching authority of the Church may raise questions. The broader social teaching of the Church, and the centrality of justice, may be new. Catholicism also may be challenging as a communal, rather than a private, faith experience.

## Three Levels of Catechesis

In addition to the touchstone of the four areas described in paragraph 75, the *General Directory for Catechesis* gives a helpful framework to determine what catechesis is needed by the baptized candidate.[1] The first level of catechesis is called the Primary Level. It is focused on an initial hearing of the Good News of Christ, and a beginning attraction to be a disciple. Often this original hearing comes earlier in life for the candidate. However, the timeliness of the candidate being moved now to pursue this direction in his or her faith life may be an opening for a deeper life of discipleship. This primary catechesis parallels the journey of a true inquirer in the precatechumenate. Catechized candidates do not need this primary catechesis.

Initiatory catechesis, the second level, has components of and a similar thrust to the catechumenate stage. As in the catechumenate, the candidate is gradually incorporated into the community and is formed in various ways into the dimensions of Christian life that are common to most Christians. The four areas of formation in the Christian life are (1) catechesis of doctrine and the mystery of salvation, (2) a transition of outlook and behavior through living the Christian life within a community, (3) engagement in liturgy, and (4) participation in apostolic service. These form the basis of initiatory catechesis. What is essential in this catechesis is that the person is engaged in a deepening

conversion of mind and behavior. This catechesis is differenti-
ated from both an initial proclamation of the Good News and
a more extensive understanding of Catholic tradition.

Continuing catechesis, the third level, moves into a
fuller understanding of dimensions of Catholic tradition, and
necessarily occurs within the framework of the community. This
catechesis, which is not primarily about incorporation into the
Christian community, most applies to the situation of the catechized candidate. Most catechized candidates who desire to live
their Christian faith within the Roman Catholic community are
already living their Christian faith. The appropriate discernment
for them involves what is needed to make this transition. Perhaps
it is getting to know members of this community through
worship, social action, faith sharing, and/or events in the community. Some of the differences between Roman Catholicism
and the tradition of the particular Christian community of the
person's formation need to be addressed. The candidate can help
name what these differences are.

## Listening to the Candidate

The essential information for discerning what is needed lies within
the candidate. First, determine whether the person is baptized, or
what may be a next step in finding out its validity, if this is necessary. Inquire about what Baptism has meant in the candidate's
life. Responses may range from never having thought about it, to
moving in and out of awareness, to being a significant part of life.
In listening, continue to use listening responses with both reflective statements and open-ended questions.

The next important area of formation to determine
is whether or not, and to what extent, the person is catechized.
The four areas of catechesis described in the period of the
catechumenate, and the three levels of catechesis presented in
the *General Directory for Catechesis*, give the discerning listener
areas to listen for in conversations with a baptized candidate.

With these frameworks in mind, the initiation minister invites the candidate to share about his or her faith background. It usually becomes clear as to whether the person is minimally acquainted with Christianity, has some Christian background without it being central in the person's life, or is quite fully living the Christian faith. What is more challenging is to determine specifically what areas need to be addressed in the formation.

## Listening with Curiosity

A helpful posture of the discerning listener is to be curious about what is shared. In other words, ask several open-ended questions. When a candidate says something like, "My grandmother took me to the Presbyterian Church when I was a child," possible follow-up questions might include "What was that like for you?" "What do you most remember?" "How has this affected your life?" Explore what they share. Inquire about additional Christian background. Then, always move to the present: "In recent years, how has Christ or the Christian faith been important for you?" "What brings you here now?"

Often candidates will cite that the spouse or fiancé is Catholic, or a child is going to be baptized or making First Communion. Don't stop here. Ask about what they want for themselves from the Church, and in their life of relationship with God.

If the candidate has been active in his or her Christian tradition, or has participated with a spouse for years in the Sunday liturgy, inquire about the meaning of moving to full Catholic communion. Is there a loss involved in moving away from the Christian community in which he or she has been a member? What is at stake with extended family members who may be part of this Christian tradition? For some candidates, this will be a challenging area with a lot of angst, or it may entail pain with some family members. Support and ongoing conversations may be needed around this shift as the candidate moves toward Reception into Full Communion.

## Readiness for Reception of the Baptized Uncatechized Candidate

A person who comes with little or no catechesis ordinarily requires a considerable time of preparation, which usually parallels the formation process of catechumens, and is coordinated with the liturgical year (401, 408). The particular time of readiness depends on conversion in mind and action, the same prerequisite a catechumen has for celebrating the Rite of Election. Over time the sponsor, catechists, and coordinator will be able to see concrete changes within the candidate. Just as it is necessary to take time with sponsors and catechumens to name these shifts, a similar process is needed for candidates. Signs of growth in the person's relationship with self, family, church, and God need to be articulated. The four areas of catechumenal formation (catechesis accommodated to the liturgical year, living Gospel values within the community, participating in appropriate liturgical prayer, and giving witness and service to others) provide a focus for naming the changes.

When readiness for Reception into Full Communion is discerned, the rite presumes a time of spiritual preparation, paralleling that of purification and enlightenment. Depending on whether the Rite of Reception will take place at or near the time of the Easter Vigil, or at another time of year, the period of this preparation may or may not coincide with Lent. If this occurs during Lent, the rites intended for the unbaptized should not be used for the baptized candidate. This is another way of respecting the baptismal status of the candidate. Rather, for example, candidates are part of the assembly praying for the elect at the scrutiny celebrations. In this way, along with the rest of the assembly, they, too, will experience the power and prayer of the scrutiny. The candidates will join with the entire community in focusing on the renewal of their baptismal covenant during the Lenten season.

The time of spiritual preparation for Reception into Full Communion may also occur at a time other than Lent. As in Lent, the focus of the preparation is a renewal of the baptismal covenant. Various prayer experiences, reflection times, or a retreat may be helpful. Whether the spiritual preparation occurs during Lent or not, the rite indicates that penitential services are part of the candidate's preparation for the celebration of the sacrament of Penance (408). This sacrament is a means of renewing one's Baptism.

Discernment about whether the candidate is ready for Reception into Full Communion is complete when the Call to Continuing Conversion is celebrated. The focus of discernment during the spiritual preparation for reception and the Sacraments of Confirmation and Eucharist will be similar to that for the elect. Individual sessions with a discerning listener and the sponsor are helpful to assist the candidate in naming his or her inner changes. How is the candidate experiencing the invitation to give his or her self over more fully to Christ? What is being let go of, or embraced? In what ways is the candidate experiencing Christ through, with, and in this community? What are the gifts the candidate is receiving in living his or her Christian faith within the Roman Catholic community?

## Readiness for Reception of the Baptized Catechized Candidate

The rite intends that the doctrinal and spiritual preparation for each baptized catechized candidate will be discerned individually (478). After assessing through conversation the areas of catechesis that are already in place, and a sense of the more that is needed, ways of attending to these are determined in dialogue. Asking the candidate what he or she believes is lacking or needed is very helpful. Often the candidate will be able to express the areas he

or she does not understand, or feels separated from or out of sync
with the rest of the community. In talking with the candidate,
some dimensions of personal life where he or she experiences a
need to change may be expressed. Without setting the time frame
at the beginning, a specific way of moving forward to attend to
these needs is designed by the catechist. This may involve some
sessions with a sponsor and a couple of catechists, and/or with
a small faith community, or endless other possibilities. Perhaps
the candidate will participate in some social action projects of the
parish, or prayer experiences. After each of these, a time of shared
reflection is beneficial. If there are any particular difficulties the
candidate has with a doctrine of the Catholic faith, with moving
away from life in a previous Christian tradition, or committing
oneself to living within the Catholic community, these need
to be discussed, prayed about, and resolved. The beliefs of the
Catholic community must be true for the candidate, who will
profess this faith at the time of Reception into Full Communion
(491). In this formation both doctrinal and spiritual dimensions
are intertwined.

A discerning listener meets periodically with the candidate to attend to his or her experience, and to help the candidate
articulate inner movements. When any blocks seem to move
away, concerns are eliminated, new understandings emerge, and
all seems in place, then it is time to discuss the time and specifics
of the Rite of Reception.

In the space between this discussion of the date and the
celebration of the Rite of Reception, the immediate spiritual
preparation occurs. With no set format or particular rituals,
spiritual preparation for the baptized catechized candidate will
be a time for him or her to attend to ways God is calling to
deeper union within the context of the Catholic tradition. The
parish may provide special vesper or word services. A penitential service may be offered to help prepare the person for the
Sacrament of Penance, which is celebrated before the Rite of
Reception (NS, 36). Quiet reflection and prayer time, whether

at the parish or in a setting away from the parish, is desirable. Hopefully, a sponsor, a discerning listener, and some members of the parish, as well as some of the candidate's family, will participate in this retreat time. The discerning listener meets individually with the candidate to give him or her the opportunity to express what is inside. This naming usually makes the inner movements clearer to the candidate.

## Discernment after the Rite of Reception into Full Communion

The rite suggests that the baptized uncatechized candidate participates in the time of mystagogy along with the newly baptized (410). There is no such statement regarding the baptized catechized candidate, perhaps because this reception will occur at another time of year. However, it is desirable to have a mystagogical reflection soon after the Rite of Reception, whenever it occurs. This is followed by as many meetings as needed, with the sponsor, the discerning listener, and/or with part of the community, to facilitate the candidate's attention to the experience of living as fully united within the Catholic community. This time also includes discerning new ways of participating in the mission of the Church. These meetings are not meant to be a burden, but are to be available as useful to support and encourage the newly received candidate in listening to the Spirit at this new moment of the Christian journey.

Discernment needs to be part of the journey to the table for the candidate in all of the various dimensions of formation, celebration of the Rite of Reception, and experience as fully united at the Eucharistic table. Through this practice of discernment, the candidate integrates the tools of discerning as a way of life.

## For Reflection

Visualize some catechized and some uncatechized candidates who have been welcomed into full communion at your parish. What are some differences you see between those who are catechized and those who are uncatechized?

Besides your regular initiation team members, who are some people or groups of people in the parish you could involve in the formation of baptized candidates?

What particular challenges do you face with baptized candidates? What resources are already in place for this ministry?

# Chapter 9

# Discernment with Children

The *Rite of Christian Initiation of Adults* provides an adaptation for children in Part II.1. The adaptation takes the adult process with stages and transitional rites as normative, and invites pastoral ministers to make them meaningful for children. The focus of initiation for children, as with adults, is conversion. This conversion is described as personal and age appropriate (253). Children, too, are on a spiritual journey. Rather than a goal of uniformity, this journey involves a slow, gradual growth, with rhythms and stages, regression and failure, as well as movements of grace. With a focus of conversion for the initiation of children, discernment is necessary. Dimensions of a child's faith journey, of the RCIA, and of concrete family and parish situations are all part of the means of discernment.

## The Initial Interview

A parent will generally stop at the parish center after Mass, say something to the priest or pastoral minister on the way out of church, call the parish office, or talk to the Catholic school principal about the Baptism or other sacraments "needed" by their child. Then, the initiation minister should set up an interview. At the beginning it is necessary to find out the particular situation of the family as well as that of the child. Is either or are both of the parents practicing Catholics? Do they support their child's Baptism and faith journey? Are siblings initiated? What is life like for the family? Are there particular struggles or family concerns? These questions may uncover some additional needs or at least give perspective to the child's family environment. In this conversation, the initiation minister listens for clues about the family situation, for example: whether parents are divorced, or if there are stepparents. Who in the family will accompany the child in their formation? Some degree of parental support is necessary. Minimally, parents are needed to get the child to initiation gatherings. Hopefully, parents will participate with the child in all aspects of initiation, from sessions to rites to parish gatherings, and will themselves participate in the life of the Church. Children are dependent on their parents (252), and parents have a great influence on the child's formation (254). In some ways the parents then become part of the initiation process, in that their own faith life has an opportunity to grow and deepen at this time.

Another important question to ask is, "Why are they seeking this now?" At times the child's friends are preparing for First Communion or Confirmation and the parents don't want the child to feel left out. Sometimes the sacraments have been missed because of moving or getting situated in a new community. The parents come forth when life has settled down enough for the family to address their faith concerns. It is also possible that a child simply has stated this desire. If the parent or child is interested in pursuing the sacraments because this is what friends or classmates are doing, begin by asking what attracts the child or what the child desires in his or her relationship with God.

Talking with the child as well as the parent is important. The child is able to state something about why he or she wants to be baptized or be involved in church. Invite the child to talk about the way he or she images God, and how the child talks to God. What does the child know about Jesus? What stories of his or her life stand out? Does the child know any other stories from the Bible? Does the child have any friends who come to this church? Does the child know anyone else who is part of the parish? This conversation gives some sense of the child's desire, as well as religious background. A free response to God's invitation is essential.

Sometimes the child will seem hesitant to talk in front of the parent. In this case, ask the parent to wait in another room while you talk with the child. At other times the child will feel much more secure with the parent there. At times, parents will be bringing the child out of a sense of duty, and, in listening to their child's desire and young faith, will find a spark to ignite their own faith. In each situation the initiation minister must continue to sense what is going on underneath the words that are spoken.

## Listen for What Is Needed

Every child is different, with a unique personality, story, background, talents, and needs. Take time beginning with this initial interview to get to know the child. The specifics of the initiation process are there to meet the needs of the child, and to support the desire for a relationship with God through the Church. Given the child's background and situation, baptized or not, catechized or not, a determination should be made about what formation will be most appropriate for the child. The options will range from a full process of initiation involving the family as well as the child, to a simpler process of initiation for a child baptized and catechized in another Christian tradition.

Initiating children is a different and larger process than putting them into religious formation in the parish or Catholic school with Catholic children preparing for sacraments.[1] The RCIA, though, conceives of the initiation process for children involving peers and other companions (254, 255). A companion family relationship, or at least the regular involvement of some of 'their peers from the parish, is important from the beginning of this process. The peers will function as parish sponsors.

The following paragraphs will attempt to provide guidance for discernment for unbaptized children of catechetical age who will engage in a full catechumenal process.

## Discernment in the Precatechumenate

The precatechumenate time is important as an environment that contrasts with the milieu of the culture. Through traditional and social media, the child is bombarded with violence, materialism, and consumerism. Often in sports the child is pressured to do well no matter what. At school the child may find his or her worth based on what is achieved or not achieved. In many families the child deals with some form of abuse. Some children have very low self esteem. The precatechumenate begins to provide a community for the child where the child feels safe and accepted for who he or she is. In this setting the child begins to let his or her real self and concerns be known.

In this time Christian values are talked about and lived. The aim of the precatechumenate for children, as with adults, is that of an initial conversion, through which the child begins moving away from wrong behavior and desires to live more closely with God (37, 42, 253). The desired conversion is not about what the child knows intellectually. The child may be able to cite story after story from Jesus' life. The child may articulate the correct moral behavior in a particular situation. Neither of these are evidence that conversion has occurred. Personal conversion means that changes in the child are happening appropriate to the child's age.

God is not spoken of very often in daily life in the child's culture. In the precatechumenate environment, though, the child is introduced not only to formal prayers, but to praying, to communication with God. God is a loving companion who is always with the child—at home, at school, in the neighborhood. The child grows in becoming acquainted with God as a personal friend. Through the stories of the child's own life, connections are made to the stories of Jesus' life. What does it mean to forgive on the playing field or when a sibling or someone at school says something hurtful? With parental involvement, this supportive faith environment gradually moves into the home as well.

Over time, catechists will hear the child sharing stories about difficult choices made, a time when he or she forgave someone, being of service without payment, or turning to God in the moment. Likewise, the desire of the child to feel closer to God will be shared. These are the signs we want to be listening for.

For Christians, Jesus is the incarnate God. The child finds Jesus to be a model. The particular stories from Jesus' life that attract the child usually depend somewhat on the child's age. Jesus is the Good Shepherd, the one who forgave sinners, who healed the ill, who welcomed children, who challenged the authorities. In working with these stories from the life of Jesus, it will be clear which ones relate to the child.

The initiation minister should periodically talk with the child. Sometimes this will be an informal "How are you doing?" as the child arrives. At other times, there may be a specific conversation or chat to ask the child to give some examples of how he or she feels a change in relationship with God, family, and friends. A child is able to state how he or she is different since beginning this process. The child also articulates a desire to be closer to God, to pray, and/or live how Jesus taught, as well as what living as part of the Church offers. When this initial conversion is present, the Rite of Acceptance is celebrated.

## Discernment in the Catechumenate

The child becomes a catechumen at the Rite of Acceptance. This rite is very meaningful. A reflection on the rite helps the child express how God acted at the rite. What was experienced with the signings of the cross on various parts of the body?

What does this say about us, and about God? What is God's personal invitation? What does it mean to be brought into the Church? What was heard? How is God's Word a gift? What more is desired from God?

The weekly dismissal after the homily, as well as dismissal from any school Masses, is an occasion for the child to recognize that something more than religious education is happening. This is a special time in the child's life. In a particular way God is speaking and acting. The community, from the Sunday assembly to the catechumenal companions to the child's class, is praying for and with the child, and lending support. This child catechumen has a special place.

The Word proclaimed in the assembly, the shared reflection on the Word after dismissal, and the catechumenal gatherings are central to the child's conversion in the catechumenate. As the liturgical year unfolds, catechists facilitate the child's finding meaning in the life, death, and Resurrection of Christ, the Paschal Mystery, and its relationship to the child's own life. While sharing appropriate Church teaching, catechists are concerned with the child integrating the values and attitudes of Jesus.

Rather than asking how much the child ought to know, catechists need to focus on the child's truly becoming part of the community of believers. How is the child participating in service dimensions of the parish? Is the child getting to know well various members of the parish? Is the child familiar with and active in the parish social events? Does the child feel at home here? Is the child assimilating the Christian lifestyle and beliefs? Initiation ministers for children need to be alert to these aspects of the child's life.

The conversion desired in the catechumenate is that of a change in outlook and behavior (75.2, 121). Cognitive formation is too often the only opportunity offered in the children's initiation experience. The RCIA calls for an inner change in the child, which is manifest in behavior. True conversion will necessarily include the child's feelings. This formation of the child's mind, heart, and spirit happens through prayer, ritual, action, sharing, and use of symbols, as well as through information. Perceptions change of life, in general, and of how one ought to live. The child is in the process of falling in love with God, of following the ways Jesus taught, of belonging to the Body of Christ, the Church. The child is engaged in service for others, and acts of justice. The child desires times of quiet prayer. Given these qualities, initiation ministers also must remember that how conversion looks is relative to the individual child according to his or her life situation and developmental capacities.

When readiness for the Easter sacraments is discerned, the child, along with the adults, celebrates the Rite of Sending for Election, and the Rite of Election. The experience of hearing testimony about God's action in oneself, and of signing the Book of the Elect in the midst of the community, is very powerful. Being called forth by the bishop in the midst of the larger assembly, and being declared elect with those from so many other parish communities, also strongly impacts the child. A mystagogical reflection on these rituals enables the child to articulate how he or she experienced God. The child often has a very strong experience of church, of unity, of covenant, of belonging. Some of this reflection and prayer may even occur with the adult elect.

## Discernment in Purification and Enlightenment

Though discernment for the Easter sacraments is complete by the Rite of Election, the period of purification and enlightenment is a time of discerning spirits more carefully. All that pertains to the adult relates to the child as well during this period.[2] The child participates in the scrutiny celebrations. Before each, the child is invited to name what holds him or her back from Christ, what he or she needs to let go of before entering the waters of Baptism. Particular images from the three scrutiny Gospels of

Christ who is the living water, the light of the world, and the resurrection and the life are helpful foci for this reflection and naming. Be sure that the children's prayers are included in the intercessions with those named by the adults. In both the preparation for the scrutinies and the reflection on the experience afterward, the family sponsor, peer companions, and/or initiation ministers assist the child in naming God's work in the experience of true freedom, healing, and being more fully joined to Christ.

Celebrating the three sacraments of initiation at the Easter Vigil with the other elect is a very significant event.[3] The child, along with parents, family sponsor, and/or peer companions, will be served by coming together afterward with adult neophytes to share how God was experienced in these powerful moments. The actions of the Spirit simply need to be articulated.

## Discernment in Mystagogy

In the time of mystagogy the neophyte child, as the adult, attends to living with this new perspective of faith, the Church, and the world (245). How is he or she different now? What is it like to process with the rest of the community to the Eucharistic table on the following Sundays? What does it mean to live Eucharist on Monday, Tuesday, and so forth? How is God's Spirit inviting him or her to live? The child, and the child's family, need this period of support to continue being attentive to God's action in the days following initiation.

Through this time of listening for God's Spirit, beginning with the initial interview and throughout the various periods and rites, the child learns the process of discernment. The child knows how to pray, to listen, and to make choices out of a loving relationship with God. From this experience the child has a strong foundation out of which to live for the rest of life.

## The Baptized Child

All kinds of pastoral situations present themselves. Some children have been baptized in another Christian tradition, with little or no catechesis. Their parents may or may not be actively participating in their Christian faith. Siblings may be active in their Christian faith, or not even baptized. Children may be presented "for the sacraments" at any age. Here, too, discernment is necessary. Though no blueprint exists for what to do in each of the situations, some concrete understandings are helpful.

Some children have been baptized as a Catholic and have had little or no catechesis. Children baptized in the Catholic Church, even if uncatechized, are not brought into full communion. They are already in communion. These children are prepared to celebrate the sacraments and participate in the life of the Church according to their age group. Rather than simply preparing for the sacraments, though, they may need some formation process to help them become active participants in the Catholic community. Remember that each child's situation is different, and so discernment is necessary to determine what will be helpful for the child. Some have had the Catholic faith as part of their family life but have not been part of a worshipping community. Others have had little exposure to the Catholic faith.

The sacramental preparation of children appropriately involves parents and peers. If they are in need of preparation for First Communion, then that preparation is taken care of and they receive it when ready. If they are in need of preparation for Confirmation, then the same would be true, but the pastor may not confirm them without explicit permission from the bishop. Or they can be prepared to be confirmed when their peers are confirmed by the bishop.

Some children have been baptized in another Christian tradition and have had little or no catechesis. As in the situation of adults, the formation process of a baptized uncatechized child will be similar to that of a catechumen, usually involving a significant amount of time.[4] Each situation is unique. Initiation ministers must glean some awareness of the child's family's faith background. Again, conversion is the focus of the journey, and is what determines the length of time needed. All of the dimensions of the catechumenate stated in paragraph 75 will be part of their formation, including that of a journey taking place in the midst of the community, catechesis accommodated to the liturgical year, participation in the Sunday liturgy, perhaps with dismissal, and service. Normally, peers and/or family sponsors will accompany the child in his or her formation. The child's baptismal status is respected, using appropriate language and celebrating the transitional rites adapted for the baptized with the adults (400, 401, 402). The child may celebrate the Rite of Reception at any time of the year.

The situation of a baptized catechized child who has been actively participating in another Christian tradition is different and needs to be addressed in a distinct manner. For example, a child who has been fully living his or her faith as a Lutheran is desiring full communion with the Catholic Church. Most often the parents will be making a similar choice. In an age appropriate way, the child will be somewhat articulate in his or her own experience of God, Jesus, values of Jesus, Church as a community of believers, significance of service to others, and prayer. Each child is unique in particular expressions of these. From conversations with the child, the initiation minister is able to glean what areas are well developed, and which need additional formation. Preparation for the sacraments will be necessary. In addition, a few sessions with an initiation minister and a community of family and peer companions may be all the additional doctrinal preparation needed. The suitable formation, though, is not equivalent to attending the parish's religious formation sessions. Assisting the child in becoming a full member of the Catholic community is not intended to be complex or difficult. However, the child's coming to full communion does need to be talked about and celebrated. The spiritual formation may include a special retreat day involving family and peer companions. The Rite of Reception is celebrated when the child is ready, and includes Confirmation and Eucharist (*National Statutes*, 32, 33, 35).

These are general norms and guidelines. Each child and each family situation are unique. Children's initiation ministers need to look for the qualities of an alive faith relationship with God, examples of values taught by Jesus being integrated into the child's life, a felt sense of belonging to and participation in the liturgy and life of the Church community. Keep in mind that formation is something beyond intellectual knowledge, and involves parents and peers. Discernment will help to identify what processes will most assist the child in becoming fully alive in his or her faith.

### For Reflection

In what ways are children who are being initiated in your parish participating in a catechumenal initiation process?

To what extent are children incorporated into the rites with adults? How does their participation affect the rest of the community?

In what ways is the conversion of the individual child discerned and attended to in your parish?

How has your parish been able to involve peers as companions in the child's initiation journey?

Chapter 10

# Initiation Ministers

## Discernment in the Parish

Saying that discernment is a way of life for all Christians is easy.
Living it is not. Concrete choices are made by looking at all the
dimensions of the choices, holding them in openness before God,
and listening for the movement of God's Spirit. The parish community is called to make choices in this way. Living as discerning
disciples is a challenge for each person individually, as well as for
the entire community. The milieu of discernment is communicated to the catechumen and candidate.

Think about what it means for a parish to discern its
choices. How central in the life of the parish is living the Paschal
Mystery celebrated in the liturgy? What values determine the
specific programs that are offered? In what ways are the poor
served? What justice-oriented concerns are supported? How are
staffing decisions made? Which announcements will be made
at Mass? How will what is printed in the Sunday bulletin be
chosen? What role does the parish council play in leading the
parish? The list of areas for discernment is long and pervasive.

What comes first, the practice of discernment in the
parish or in the initiation process? It is true that the attitude of
discernment grows in one as it does in the other. However, in
many parishes, when initiation ministers see that conversion is
the focus of the RCIA and move to discern readiness before celebrating a rite, the awareness of discernment begins to spill over
into other areas of parish life. Following a way of discernment
in initiation ministry calls all of us to live in greater truth with

God, with ourselves, and in all of our relationships. Choices are discerned out of Gospel values.

## Personal Discernment

The parish, through its prayerful community life, liturgy, and general tenor, supports individuals in their personal discernment. A variety of personal concerns may call for discernment. These range from relational situations with one's spouse, children, parents, or family of origin to friends, coworkers, and/or fellow parishioners. Choices present themselves about what is the appropriate ministerial involvement in the parish, place of employment, and whether or not to move. Some persons are called in a more dramatic way to give service to the poor or work for justice concerns. Others desire more time in quiet prayer. At times negative behavior or a compulsion may need attention. Some of the discernment areas involve struggle, letting go, or doing something that is challenging or even painful. Others may occur quite easily and with seemingly little effort.

## The Parish Initiates

Initiation is central to parish life and is part of the Church's liturgy. The RCIA specifies that the responsibility for initiation belongs to the entire community (9). Everyone in the community is viewed as an initiation minister. These are not only words. They speak a truth. During the precatechumenate members of the parish are involved with inquirers through informal conversations, in their homes and neighborhoods, and at functions in the parish community (9.1). From the beginning of the catechumenate, the community's participation in the various rites and liturgies is essential (9.2–5). Each parish, whether very large or quite small, must work to involve the community in its proper role.

Some individuals will be called to minister with those being initiated in a particular way: as a coordinator, catechist, sponsor, liturgist, presider, or as a hospitality minister. Though the whole parish are truly initiation ministers, some members of the parish assume responsibility for the implementation of the initiation process. The initiation ministers should be formed in such a way that they are able to discern in their personal lives, as members of the parish community participating in regular parish life decisions, and with those being initiated. These initiation ministers also develop their ability to discern by listening to the Spirit's revelation to them through their ministry.

## God Speaks to the Ministers

Though both ordinary life and weekly initiation gatherings are full, a real gift is available in taking time to do some discerning listening as a ministry team. Many initiation ministers are becoming quite proficient at listening for movements of God's Spirit within catechumens and candidates. A further and important invitation is to take time to notice God's Spirit at work in themselves in this ministry. For example, a few initiation ministers gather after each session. In addition to describing the experience of leading a session, noting what seems to be happening in the inquirers, catechumens, or candidates, and giving feedback to the catechist, initiation ministers could share how each experienced God's Spirit moving in them. For the moment, the focus shifts to the individual initiation ministers. At a monthly gathering of catechists, in addition to talking about catechumens, candidates, their needs, and upcoming sessions, reflection time could be taken for sharing how God has been working in them as they prepare and lead a session. In small parishes, this may even be done as an individual reflection if initiation ministers are scarce.

## Yearly Team Reflection

Certain times of the year present specific opportunities for the initiation ministers to discern as well. For example, after the mystagogical Easter season, initiation ministers attend to how the Spirit has impacted them in the past year. How has their own faith been affected by the neophytes' journeys? It is easy to keep the focus on the newly initiated and their remarkable stories of faith. The initiation ministers may easily talk about how the neophytes changed, how God filled them in Baptism, how the Spirit is acting in them. But this time of year also affords an opportunity for initiation ministers to notice how their own faith has been affected by their participation in the journey of the initiated.

Another advantageous discernment time is soon after Pentecost. The initiation ministers might gather for a dinner and evening of reflection, or a retreat day/afternoon away. Try to be sure this is experienced as a time of refreshment and renewal, rather than as an additional task. Social time, unscheduled time, and a shared meal might be incorporated into the retreat. The Pentecost reading, Acts 2:1–11, can provide a helpful springboard for reflective questions like "What are the gifts you have received?" "What face of God have you seen manifest?" The second Pentecost reading, 1 Corinthians 12:3b –7, 12 –13, lends itself to the question, "What are the new gifts coming alive in you?"

Another way initiation ministers might be aware of the Spirit's activity is to ask themselves, "How am I different now from a year ago as the result of my involvement in initiation ministry?" Giving voice to these experiences with at least one other person usually leads to a fuller appreciation and recognition of what God is doing in one's own life.

Initiation ministers might also look at their lives beyond the catechumenate ministry. In the past year, what are the ways the Spirit has been operating through family, work, or other parish ministry? One way to do this is to encourage each initiation minister to develop a time line for the past twelve months, marking the line in monthly sections. Reflectively look back over the year. Below the line write family, work, or parish events, and any additional significant remembrances. Then, go back over the year, and write above the line how the Spirit was active in these experiences.

These reflection possibilities are meant to assist initiation ministers in continuing to become aware of the many ways the Spirit is alive and acting in them. These are exercises, so to speak, to build up the muscles of the practice of discernment.

## Developing Parish Initiation Ministers

Periodically, at least yearly, initiation ministers must discern the parish's next steps in more fully becoming an initiating community. Some parishes have already moved to a year-round process. Others are still considering this direction. Some parishes need to develop their initiation ministry with children, or with the already baptized.

In addition, this is a good time to ask how the ministry team will continue to develop. Perhaps more ministers are needed to meet the needs of a more diversified initiation process. One resource for new initiation ministers is found in recent sponsors, who seem to understand the initiation process. Various other parishioners may also be invited to consider a specific ministry. Some initiation ministers may no longer experience energy to continue. Other initiation ministers who are resistant to the real understanding and practice of initiation ministry may need to be challenged. The focus of any of these considerations is not what one person thinks or feels versus another. The underlying question is, "What is God's invitation to you and to the parish's initiation ministry at this time?" How are the initiation ministers listening to the Spirit? In what ways is someone locked into his or her own position? Consider this image: place each of the initiation ministers, these questions, and the people being served in one's hands. Then, open these hands in prayer, and ask God, "What do you want?" After all, it is God's grace that is working through all that the initiation ministers and parish does.

## Initiation Teams Get Stuck

Sometimes real struggles, named or unnamed, exist regarding those involved in initiation ministry. Many initiation teams have taken a number of years to form. However, once formed, they become set in stone: "We do the process 'his' or 'her' way." Changes become next to impossible. Though some of the initiation ministers may understand the vision of moving to a year-round process, others control it by saying, "We've always done it this way, and it works." Another reason given is "We are already overworked. How can we add a new dimension?" Yet, even when the possibility is mentioned of expanding the initiation team members or diversifying without everyone doing everything, there is reticence. Initiation ministers need to remember that they are invited to continual conversion and discernment as are the catechumens and candidates.

Some initiation ministers get into routines that become sacred cows. One person always giving the same presentation may work well, or it may seem stale, or even biased: "I don't want to invite others to participate in initiation because we have it all worked out with who does what in the process." Underneath this posture is a desire to control and we must be careful of this attitude. Sometimes there is a fear of doing something different, or the lack of time or creativity to envision new possibilities.

Perhaps someone leading sessions in one of the stages has gifts that would better fit into another part of the process. For example, a person leading a precatechumenate session takes up most of the time "teaching" or giving his or her opinion, rather than facilitating discussion and sharing from the inquirers. This presenter may be a wonderful teacher whose gifts would serve others better in the catechumenate. Often persons are unaware of their biases and behaviors.

What is the invitation of discernment in these situations? Once again, discernment involves a willingness to hold all before God in honesty and listen for God's response. Sometimes, this may lead to the coordinator or someone else having an individual conversation with an initiation minister to talk about a concern. When doing this, it is not enough to speak the truth. The truth must always be spoken with love and care. Remember again the image of holding all in one's hands before God and asking, "What do you want?" Arriving at this place of openness usually takes time.

Getting further training at a workshop provides a stepping off point for moving forward in a fresh way. A new understanding and concrete ideas may be the catalyst and provide the assistance needed to make a shift. When initiation ministers together hear the same vision presented at a workshop, seize the moment for conversation about how initiation ministry functions in the parish. Rather than changing everything at once, it is realistic to set two or three goals for the coming year.

The initiation ministers may wish to gather specifically for a time of their own discernment. Any discernment needs to occur within the context of prayer, asking God for an openness and willingness to listen. A beginning place could be for each initiation minister to note, perhaps in writing, his or her own desires in this ministry and reasons that support this. The individuals must be free to express their real feelings, hesitations, and hopes. Each person thus becomes aware of how strong the attachment is to this position and asks God for a willingness to be open and truly hear others. Then there could be a sharing of what each has written. After all have shared, each initiation minister might complete the phrase "What I hear us saying is . . . " This will lead to some discussion. It is often advantageous to go away and reflect and pray, possibly gathering again to dialogue further in a week. The initiation ministers may be able to do this process on their own, or may need a facilitator.

## Parish Initiation Needs

Larger parish initiation concerns are part of discernment. In considering how the initiation process is appropriated in a local parish, the RCIA's goal of conversion is the touchstone. Discernible areas include the following: Is God calling the larger parish to be more involved in initiation? In what ways is apostolic service incorporated into the initiation process? Does the parish experience one initiation process that includes both adults and children? How does the parish distinguish between catechumens, uncatechized candidates, and those who are catechized? Given that the Church's liturgical life is ongoing, and that the Spirit acts at various times, is God calling the parish to an ongoing initiation process? How is conversion discerned and valued in the initiation process? What are the next steps in incorporating the RCIA's vision of initiation in this parish?

Though there are many goals for the vision of the RCIA to be a reality, exactly how this initiation process happens or who will be involved will be different in each parish community. Parishes vary greatly in size, locale, culture, and resources. With the real "givens" in a situation, and with the vision of the RCIA before them, initiation ministers are able to discern with an open heart what is truly possible in this parish.

### For Reflection

How is discernment lived in the parish at large? Give one concrete example of a parish discernment that has occurred.

Who are some of the people in your parish who seem to be discerning persons? What do you see in them that tells you this?

What issues of discernment lie before your initiation team members? What is your first step in addressing these issues?

*Appendixes*

# *Appendix 1: The Initial Interview*

This interview could occur in the inquirer's home or in a parish setting. The environment should be welcoming and inviting, avoiding the formality of sitting across a desk or table from one another.

1. Greet and welcome the inquirer.

2. Get to know the inquirer.
   In discussing the following areas, remember to respond with reflective statements that include content and feelings, and to use open-ended questions that invite a fuller response. Ask about
   a. family, work or school, home—if in geographical area;
   b. the reason for inquiring, and why at this time;
   c. what the person is looking for and/or desiring for self;
   d. religious upbringing and background, including Baptism;
   e. relationship with God through the years and at this time; and
   f. how inquiring in the Catholic Church relates to spouse and/or children, and whether there is family support. At this initial meeting, pay attention to information gleaned regarding former marriage situations without discussing annulments unless the question is raised by the inquirer.

3. Talk with the inquirer about the initiation process.
   Communicate that this adult faith journey
   a. is individualized and involves personal faith in relationship to life experience;
   b. takes time and is open-ended;
   c. occurs in the context of community;
   d. happens in stages with periodic liturgical celebrations; and
   e. involves ongoing discernment, including individual conferences and team discernment.

4. Give specific information about inquiry sessions and future catechumenate sessions. Include time and place, and a sense of what to expect with each. Stress that the time of both is open-ended, and initiation ministers will be listening with the person for when the readiness is there for movement to the next stage. The precatechumenate is a time of exploration with no commitment.

5. Mention that a sponsor will be needed when moving on to the catechumenate. Ask if they know someone in the parish (not a family member) who should be considered.

6. Ask how all of this sounds to them, and invite comments and concerns.

7. Get any specific information needed (name, address, spouse, children, Baptism date and place, and so forth).

8. Express gratitude for coming and sharing, and extend an invitation to the next inquiry session.

# Appendix 2: The Interview during the Precatechumenate

This interview occurs several weeks before the Rite of Acceptance into the Order of Catechumens, when the precatechumenate leaders see signs that the initial conversion is happening. The areas of discussion come out of the prerequisites for this rite stated in paragraph 42. A designated initiation minister conducts the interview in an appropriate setting; that is, private, inviting, with no desk or table between the inquirer and interviewer. The interviewer uses appropriate discerning listening skills to enable the inquirer to talk at a deeper level about inner awarenesses. Each of the person's responses may be delved into, following the inquirer's lead and willingness to engage.

1. The interviewer begins with a greeting, welcome, and expression of gratitude for coming.

2. There is a moment of prayer. For example, "Let's take a moment of quiet to recall we are in God's presence, and are here because of God's invitation. (*Pause for a moment.*) God, thank you for your presence, and ways you invite us and call us to you. Be with us now. Help us listen together to your action in the life of (inquirer's name). Guide our time together. In Jesus' name, we pray. Amen."

3. The interviewer names this as a time of listening to God's actions within the inquirer, with the intention of discerning the appropriate timing for movement to the catechumenate.

4. Invitations to talk about areas named in paragraph 42 follow:
   a. How has this time of precatechumenate/inquiry been for you?

b. Are you noticing any changes happening in your relationship with your spouse/children?

c. Have you found that you are any different at work (or school)
than you used to be?

d. Are there any changes in yourself, in how you feel as
a person?

e. How has your relationship with God been affected by your
coming to the inquiry sessions?

f. Can you talk about any ways your prayer has changed?

g. Do you have a sense of how God is leading you, or where
God might be inviting you to grow or change?

h. How are you coming to appreciate what church is?

i. Do you have any questions or concerns you'd like
to discuss?

5. If an annulment is needed and has not yet been discussed,
and the inquirer is interested in pursuing membership in the
Catholic Church, then the inquirer should be encouraged to talk
with the appropriate person to begin the annulment process.

6a. If the inquirer, initiation ministers, or interviewer has concerns about the person moving on to the catechumenate, these
would be talked about in conjunction with responses the person
has made to the above questions. There may be an agreement
about coming together again in another month or six weeks to
see what's happening in the person then. The interviewer concludes the conference.

6b. If the inquirer, initiation ministers, and interviewer sense
from the sharing during the inquiry sessions and in the interview
that the needed initial conversion is taking place, then the following areas are discussed:

1. Inquirers are invited to talk about their readiness and desire
to move into the catechumenate.

2. The interviewer then talks about ritualizing this moment with the Rite of Acceptance into the Order of Catechumens. This will be the first time the inquirer is brought publicly into the liturgical assembly. The catechumenate is an official order in the Church. A catechumen has the right to Catholic marriage and burial. Catechumens participate weekly in the Liturgy of the Word and are dismissed after the homily to share, discuss, and learn more about our tradition. The Word proclaimed each Sunday in the liturgical assembly is the source of our formation and learning. By participating in this rite, the inquirer is professing a desire to earnestly pursue the Catholic faith, and is committed to coming weekly, except for times of illness or being out of town. At this time, the desire exists for full participation in the Catholic faith.

3. If one has not yet been chosen, the interviewer talks about having a sponsor and what a sponsor is. Further conversation follows about sponsors available from the parish community and/or a nonfamily member the inquirer may know.

4. Steps about connecting with a sponsor are decided, if this is not already in place. Particulars about the timing of the Rite of Acceptance are discussed.

7. The interviewer concludes the conference, expressing gratitude for the inquirer's coming and honest sharing about God's inner movement.

# Appendix 3: The First Interview during the Catechumenate

After ten or twelve weeks in the catechumenate, the coordinator invites the catechumen to a personal conference with the designated discerning listener to continue to discern and articulate God's inner movement. The predetermined conference time is usually forty-five to sixty minutes. The discerning listener attends to the areas named in paragraph 75. In hearing what is said, the listener helps the catechumen notice the shifts and stirrings of the heart, as well as outer manifestations. The listener also brings forth initiation ministers' concerns. There is a similar format to earlier conferences with the exception that the areas generally come out of what the catechumen says, not necessarily in the order named here.

1. Greeting, welcome, and expression of gratitude for this time together.

2. A time of prayer. For example, "Let's pause for a few minutes of quiet to sense God's presence with us here. Then I'll pray aloud. Feel free to add your prayer either aloud or in silence. I'll then conclude our time of prayer. Let's begin with some silence to listen within. (*Pause.*) 'God, be with (name of catechumen) and me as we attend to your action in his/her life. Open each of us to hear and see what you want us to notice. Guide our time together.' (*Pause for catechumen's prayer.*) 'We bring ourselves to you, for your honor and glory, now and forever. In Jesus' name, we pray. Amen.' "

3. The listener begins by asking how this time of catechumenate is for the person. What have the catechumenate sessions been like for the catechumen? The listener continues to delve into the responses with reflective statements and inviting questions.

4. How is it for the catechumen to participate in the Liturgy of the Word with the sponsor and be dismissed? What has been the catechumen's experience as the Word is further opened up each week?

5. The listener asks the catechumen to articulate how relationship with Christ is growing, and the impact this makes in relationships with family, neighborhood, work or school, and self. How is change or growth happening?

6. In what ways is the catechumen feeling part of the Church?

7. The listener also explores the area of apostolic service with the catechumen. Is the catechumen involved or interested in any particular service? What options are available?

8. How is the sponsor relationship developing?

9. Are the catechumen's needs being met? Are questions being answered? Are there any concerns within self, with family, or with the initiation process?

10. If concerns have been expressed by initiation ministers, then the listener must bring these forth at the moment that feels appropriate. These concerns may be talked about in conjunction with what the catechumen shares.

11. Are there areas in the catechumen's life where God seems to be inviting a change? In terms of the inner spiritual life, for what does the catechumen want to ask God? Invite the catechumen to spend some time expressing this desire to God in prayer during the coming week.

12. The listener closes the conference with a moment of appreciation, acknowledging what has been shared. The listener offers future conference possibilities.

## Appendix 4: The Interview before the Rite of Election

This forty-five to sixty-minute conference occurs several weeks before the Rite of Election, with the intention of receiving the catechumen's self-understanding and experience for the larger discernment process. The interviewer will want to determine to what extent the four areas named in paragraph 75 have been and have become part of the catechumen's life. Also, the interviewer is intent on discerning how the conversion in mind and in action named in paragraph 120 has occurred. At the time of setting up the conference, the interviewer informs the catechumen that this input will be represented by the listener to the team in the discernment process. Before the conference, the interviewer contacts various initiation ministers and sponsors to glean areas of concern that may need to be discussed. During the conference, the interviewer ascertains confidentiality needs of the catechumen and assures this in any specified areas.

As the catechumen speaks of what is happening within himself or herself, the listener responds with reflective statements and inviting questions, in particular noticing feelings, to enable the catechumen to more fully express what is inside. In following areas named by the catechumen, the conversation will not necessarily occur in the order given.

1. Greeting, welcome, and expression of gratitude for coming to talk.

2. A time of prayer. For example, "As we begin, let's take a moment of quiet to become conscious of God's presence with us. Then I'll pray aloud. You may add your prayer either aloud or in the silence of your heart. After a few moments I'll conclude our time of prayer. Let's begin just sensing God's presence with us

here. (*Pause for a couple minutes.*) 'Gracious God, you have called us each by name and we are yours. We come together to discern whether you are inviting (name of catechumen) to more time in the catechumenate or to the Easter sacraments. Help us to truly listen to your voice, and to speak and hear your truth in one another. Guide our conversation.' (*Pause for catechumen's prayer.*) 'We offer you our lives, and we pray in the name of Jesus, now and forever. Amen.' "

3. State that this conference is part of the discernment process before the celebration of the Rite of Election. Give a brief explanation of the importance of discernment and why this is occurring before the Rite of Election. Clarify the steps of the discernment process and invite any question or response from the catechumen.

4. The listener begins with a general question, inviting what has been happening within the person since the last conversation. The listener continues to follow the lead of this response with reflective statements and inviting questions.

5. The listener continues to invite expression of movement happening within the catechumen in the person's various relationships, in prayer, in inner self, and in any particular areas of struggle named in the previous conversation.

6. What has been the catechumen's experience of apostolic service? How has this impacted him or her?

7. Is the catechumen aware of inner struggles where it feels as if God is pulling in a different direction than the person wants to go? Or is the catechumen feeling somewhat pliable in God's hands? These questions are an attempt to uncover where conversion has happened and where it may still need to occur. Is the catechumen willing to talk with God about any resis-

tances? Invite the catechumen to name what he or she would want to pray for in this regard.

8. Discuss any concerns you or the team members have with the catechumen. Remember to give concrete examples or behaviors to back up the concerns. Express them in a way that invites the catechumen to talk about what may be going on underneath the behaviors and not as an accusation.

9. Ask how the catechumen is sensing his or her readiness for the celebration of the Rite of Election and desire for the Easter sacraments. Explore the response with the catechumen.

10. Ask if you may share the basic content of what has been shared in this conversation with other initiation ministers within a prayerful discernment, or if there is something he or she wishes to be confidential.

11. Tell the catechumen when you will get back to him or her after the discernment. Express gratitude for the honest sharing.

12. End with a prayer of gratitude for all God is doing in the catechumen.

13. Spend a few minutes after the conference noting your impressions, or any specific things you want to bring to the discernment from this conference.

# Appendix 5: The Discernment Day before the Rite of Election

The coordinator, initiation members, sponsors, and pastor come together for a day of discernment several weeks before the First Sunday of Lent when the Rite of Election will be celebrated. At least a week before this gathering, the coordinator asks each sponsor to prepare and bring some testimony about his or her catechumen in relationship to the four areas of paragraph 75, and the sponsor's sense of the catechumen's conversion process. Either through written word or (preferably) through personal presence, the sponsor as the "witness to the candidates' moral character, faith, and intention" (10) needs to be included in the discernment.

In preparation for this day, the coordinator may also invite members of the local community named by a catechumen to give input about evidence of his or her conversion. This testimony is compiled for each catechumen before the discernment day begins.

The discernment setting is prayerful, and includes appropriate environment with a lit candle and Bible. The day begins with communal prayer.

## 1. Communal Prayer

*Leader:* We gather together today to prayerfully discern, to listen with our hearts to how God is moving in the catechumens' lives, and whether there is evidence that God is electing them for the initiation sacraments this Easter. Let us ready our hearts to be attuned to God's Spirit.

Gathering Hymn: Inviting the Spirit's presence, for example, "Send Us Your Spirit."

Opening Prayer:

*Leader:* Gracious God, do send your Spirit to us for the important work we are about to do today. Open our minds and hearts and beings to hear and see what you want us to. Move us as you will. Give us your gift of wisdom as we listen for your movement in each of our catechumens. Speak through us and among us. We ask this, in the name of Jesus.

*All:* Amen.

The Word of God:

Colossians 3:12–17   or   Ephesians 3:14–21

Sung Response:

for example, Psalm 25

Silent Prayer

*Leader:* Let us join together in praying as Jesus taught us:

Our Father . . .

*Leader:* May our God, who has given us these catechumens as gifts of grace, continue to inspire our lives to bring these gifts to fulfillment, and bless us always.

*All:* Amen.

*Leader:* Let us offer one another the sign of Christ's peace.

2. The coordinator (or whoever is designated to lead the day) describes the discernment process that will be used, and also states that whatever will be shared by anyone is to remain confidential and not talked about outside of the discernment experience.

3. The Discernment Process

a.   The coordinator presents a catechumen by first giving his or her name, and any pertinent information, which might include how long the person has been a catechumen, faithfulness in participating in catechumenal sessions, and the coordinator's sense of the person's journey.

b.   The sponsor then gives the witness testimony to how the four areas of the catechumenate as named in paragraph 75 are lived out in the catechumen's life, and the noticed changes in him or her from the beginning until the present. If the sponsor is not present, the written testimony of the sponsor is read aloud.

c.   Written testimony of other members of the local community is read aloud.

d.   Catechists and other initiation ministers are invited to give input.

e.   The interviewer then gives the general sense of how the catechumen experiences his or her conversion process and sense of readiness to move toward the sacraments of initiation.

f.   The coordinator asks all to pause and listen within whether there seem to be signs of God's electing this person, or whether there are questions and concerns. The coordinator invites participants in this discernment to visualize this catechumen and themselves in God's presence, and prays, "Spirit of God, speak in us the truth you want us to see about (name of catechumen)." Several minutes of silent listening follow.

g.   The coordinator invites statements of what has been heard in the silence, of affirmation and/or of concern.

h.   The coordinator summarizes what has been stated. If the catechumen has been affirmed as having evidence of being elected by God, that is named. If there is disagreement, more discussion and prayer are needed until a movement in one direction becomes clear. If all agree that concerns and hesitations exist, then these are named clearly so that the interviewer may go back and speak to the person.

i.    Then the coordinator begins this same process again with the name of the next catechumen until all have been presented.

4. At the conclusion, the coordinator invites all present to a few minutes of silence to take note of the experience of the Spirit's presence during this day. After this time of quiet, the coordinator invites any who wish to share how the Spirit was present.

5. The day concludes with a time of prayer.

The Closing Prayer:
Each catechumen is named and prayed for in silence.
After all catechumens have been named, anyone who wishes, offers a prayer aloud.

Concluding Prayer:
*Leader:* Gracious Spirit of God, we thank you for your presence here among us, and for gifting your Church with these men and women you call to yourself. We offer you our gratitude for your goodness and love. We make this prayer through the Holy Spirit, now and forever.

*All:* Amen.

Closing Hymn:
A hymn of praise, for example, "All the Ends of the Earth."

6. The coordinator reminds those present that what has been stated by anyone is to be kept confidential, and expresses gratitude to all present for coming and for their participation.

# Appendix 6: *The Training of Team Members and Sponsors in the Way of Discerning Listening*

Below I describe elements that are important to develop the skills of discerning listening in team members and sponsors. Each local situation will differ regarding the number of training sessions, and what to include. I personally believe it would be helpful to have at least three sessions to give participants time to practice between the sessions.

**Session I**

1. An overview of discernment. (See chapter 1.) Points to include are
   a. discernment is a listening within for God's way;
   b. discernment is a necessary part of living as a disciple;
   c. we hand on this way of discernment to our inquirers and catechumens;
   d. the *Rite of Christian Initiation of Adults* calls us to discern throughout the process, before the Rite of Acceptance, and in particular before the Rite of Election;
   e. an understanding of the human person includes feelings, "shoulds," inner tapes, resistance, and desire;
   f. God communicates through real human experience; and
   g. ways to understand the meaning of God's will.

2. Discerning listening. (See Chapter 2.) Points to include are
   a. discerning listening listens to and with another for God's movement;
   b. discerning listening trusts that the answers and needed resources are within the person;

    c.   discerning listening facilitates the person in finding God's truth inside;

    d.   discerning listening aids the person in noticing thoughts, feelings, and desires; and

    e.   discerning listening supports the person in attending to inner truth.

3. Presenting specific listening skills. (See chapter 3.)

    a. Responding with statements that reflect back meaning.

       1. Give examples of statements that reflect back meaning. Do this as a role play with one person speaking, and one person reflecting back. Use the following and/or your own examples:

       *Speaker 1:* I rushed to work this morning, then barely had time to eat at home before coming to this meeting.
       *Listener 1:* You had a very full day going from one thing to the next.

       *Speaker 2:* At work today I was accused by a coworker of saying something to my boss about this coworker that I did not say.
       *Listener 2:* Today was a difficult day at work since you were falsely accused of saying something you didn't.

       2. Divide those present into groups of two and have them practice with one another. First, have one speak and the other listen for five minutes using statements that reflect content. Then reverse roles for five minutes.

    b. Responding with statements, words, or phrases that reflect back feeling.

       1. Give examples of statements that reflect back feeling. Do this as a role-play with one person speaking, and another reflecting back. Use the following and/or your own examples.

*Speaker 1:* I don't know what to do about my teenager. He was sent home from school today for disrupting the class again!
*Listener 1:* You are quite concerned, and at a loss of what to say or do.

*Speaker 2:* A car turning left nearly hit me just before I arrived here. My heart is still pounding.
*Listener 2:* You're feeling frightened.

2. Again, divide those present into groups of two, and have them practice with one another, giving reflective statements of feelings. Do this for five minutes, and then change roles for the next five minutes.

c. Come back together as a large group. Invite participants to name what it was like for them as speakers to be listened to in this way. Then invite participants to name their experience as listeners to listen in this way.

4. Encourage participants to practice these skills with family, friends, or coworkers until the next session. Some participants may even want to meet together in pairs or talk on the phone to practice these skills. In particular, encourage them to give reflective responses that include feelings.

**Session II**
1. This session begins by inviting feedback from the listening experiences since the last session. What was it like for them to do this type of listening? What are they learning about themselves?

2. Give examples of other kinds of responses that do not reflect back, using the following categories:
   a.  advice-giving;
   b.  avoiding pain and painful feelings;
   c.  spiritualizing, especially with clichés; and
   d.  giving suggestions from one's own life.

See chapter 3 for some examples, or you may use your own. I suggest doing these in a demonstration role-play and inviting the participants to name how what you are doing is different from reflecting back. The more experiential this session, the better it will be understood. Then invite the participants to talk in small groups (or with one other person) about which of these types of responses they find themselves using.

3. Divide into groups of four. In each group, designate a speaker, a listener, and two observers. Have one person speak about an experience or aspect of his or her present life that is important. Have another be the listener who gives responses that primarily reflect feeling. Do this for ten to fifteen minutes. Then, take a few moments of quiet, inviting each of the four to notice his or her experience. Process the experience within each group for about fifteen minutes, using the following order: The listener tells how he or she felt, and what he or she feels good about saying, or would want to say differently. Then, the speaker says what was helpful or not helpful in the responses given. The two observers then give examples of reflective and other responses that were made. The goal is for more self-awareness in the person who is the listener.

4. Stay in the same groups. Repeat step 3 with a new speaker and a new listener.

5. Bring the whole group together. Ask what is being learned about the listening process. Then invite participants to name what is being discovered about themselves as listeners.

6. Until this point we have been responding through statements, phrases, and words, and especially noticing feelings. Another aspect of discerning listening is asking inviting questions that help the person explore his or her experience. Through role-plays, present various kinds of questions: those that involve fact,

those that cause one to analyze, and those that help a person delve further into experience. (See chapter 3.) Invite participants to name the difference in what happens as a result of these kinds of questions.

7. Divide into groups of two with one speaker and one listener. One person speaks for five minutes about a significant experience involving feelings. The listener responds, using inviting questions. Then the roles are reversed.

8. Repeat step 5.

9. Before the next gathering, participants are to practice listening with one other person for thirty minutes. They are to listen and use both kinds of responses: reflecting back feelings and asking inviting questions. Have them find a partner and discuss when they will meet.

**Session III**

1. Begin by inviting participants to name their experience of listening when using reflective responses and inviting questions.

2. Again, divide into groups of four, with a speaker, listener, and two observers in each group. Invite the speaker to share for ten to fifteen minutes some way he or she experienced God this week outside of Mass or any parish activity. The listener uses both reflective responses and inviting questions. The observers notice the effect of various responses the listener makes. When finished, pause for a few minutes of reflection. In each group, the listener speaks first of his or her awareness and feelings during the experience and in reflecting back on it. Then the speaker gives specific input about various responses the listener gave that were or were not helpful. The observers then state what they noticed, giving concrete examples.

3. Invite all participants to reflect for a few moments about something that lately has been in their mind and heart. Specifically ask them to note their feelings. Then have them pair off, and share this experience. First, one person speaks and the other listens for about twenty minutes. Then the roles are reversed. When they return, invite them to reflect on their experience.

    a. What was it like when you were the speaker? How did it feel to tell your experience? How did you feel having someone listen to you? Invite a sharing in the large group.

    b. What was it like when you were the listener? How did it feel to have someone share something meaningful with you? Invite a sharing in the large group.

4. Invite each participant to reflect on one or two things to which he or she wants to be attentive in order to grow as a listener. Have the participants share this with one other person.

5. Ask if there are suggestions or any desire for future meetings and/or practice sessions with discerning listening. Determine any next steps.

6. Express gratitude to participants for their time and engagement in this listening ministry.

# Notes

*Introduction*

1. For a discussion of considerations in initiating the already baptized Christians of another faith tradition and uncatechized Catholics, see Ron Oakham, *One At the Table: The Reception of Baptized Christians.* (Chicago: Liturgy Training Publications, 1995).

*Chapter 1*

1. In his *Spiritual Exercises*, St. Ignatius uses the image of an "angel of light" in the discernment of spirits for someone with a second-week experience. See no. 332 in Louis J. Puhl, SJ, *The Spiritual Exercises of St. Ignatius.* (Chicago: Loyola University Press, 195), 1.

2. National Conference of Catholic Bishops. *Rite of Christian Initiation of Adults.* (Chicago: Liturgy Training Publications, 1988). References to materials from this rite will be given in parentheses.

*Chapter 2*

1. Throughout his *Spiritual Exercises*, Ignatius urges attention to movements of the Spirit. See especially nn. 6 and 17 in *The Spiritual Exercises of St. Ignatius.*

*Chapter 3*

1. For a helpful resource in various aspects of listening skills, see Robert Bolton, PhD, *People Skills: How to Assert Yourself, Listen to Others, and Resolve Conflicts.* (New York: A Touchstone Book published by Simon & Schuster, Inc., 1986).

2. The study referred to is described in Mary Field Belenky, Blythe McVicker Clinchy, Nancy Rule Goldberger, and Jill Mattuck Tarule, *Women's Ways of Knowing: The Development of Self, Voice, and Mind* (New York: Basic Books, Inc., 1986), pp. 52–62. Although this book cites the experience of women, from my ministry of doing spiritual direction, I believe this not only applies to women but is a human reality.

*Chapter 6*

**1.** Edward Yarnold, SJ. *The Awe-Inspiring Rites of Initiation: the Origins of the R.C.I.A.* (Collegeville, Minnesota: The Liturgical Press, 1994), p. 20.

*Chapter 8*

**1.** Chapter 2 of the *General Directory for Catechesis* presents a clear understanding of the three types of catechesis.

*Chapter 9*

**1.** For a comprehensive, readable, and helpful understanding of why the initiation of children is different from formation for sacraments that Catholic children receive, and dimensions of the initiation of children, read *The Christian Initiation of Children: Hope for the Future* by Robert D. Duggan and Maureen A. Kelly. (New York: Paulist Press, 1991).

**2.** In "The Penitential Rite (Scrutiny) for Children" (*Catechumenate*, November 1999), Rita Burns Senseman explores the question of whether children should participate in the scrutinies with the adult elect, or celebrate the Penitential Rite for Children, given in the rite. My pastoral experience and theological understanding supports including children in the scrutiny celebrations. This more fully expresses the truth that there is one catechumenate, in which both adults and children participate.

**3.** The rite is clear that the three sacraments of initiation are to be celebrated at the same celebration, and in the order of Baptism, Confirmation, then Eucharist for all children of catechetical age. (NS, 14).

**4.** For a fuller explanation, read chapter 8 on the initiation of the baptized candidate in this book.

# Bibliography

Belenky, Mary Field, Blythe McVicker Clinchy, Nancy Rule Goldberger, and Jill Mattuck Tarule. *Women's Ways of Knowing: The Development of Self, Voice, and Mind.* New York: Basic Books, Inc., 1986.

Bolton, Robert. *People Skills: How to Assert Yourself, Listen to Others, and Resolve Conflicts.* New York: A Touchstone Book, Simon & Schuster, Inc., 1986.

Congregation for the Clergy, *General Directory for Catechesis.* United States Catholic Conference, Washington, DC, 1998.

Duggan, Robert D. and Kelly, Maureen A. *The Christian Initiation of Children: Hope for the Future.* New York: Paulist Press, 1991.

Hart, Thomas N. *The Art of Christian Listening.* New York: Paulist Press, 1980.

*Journey to the Fullness of Life: A Report on the Implementation of the Rite of Christian Initiation of Adults in the United States.* United States Catholic Conference, Washington, DC, 2000.

National Conference of Catholic Bishops. *Rite of Christian Initiation of Adults.* Chicago: Liturgy Training Publications, 1988.

Oakham, Ron. *One At the Table: The Reception of Baptized Christians.* Chicago: Liturgy Training Publications, 1995.

Puhl, Louis J., SJ. *The Spiritual Exercises of St. Ignatius.* Chicago: Loyola University Press, 1951.

Senseman, Rita Burns. "The Penitential Rite (Scrutiny) for Children" in *Catechumenate: A Journal of Christian Initiation,* Chicago: Liturgy Training Publications, Volume 21, Number 6, November 1999.

Yarnold, Edward, SJ. *The Awe-Inspiriting Rites of Initiation: The Origins of the R.C.I.A.* Collegeville, Minnesota: The Liturgical Press, 1994.